BITE-SIZED

FRENCH PASTRIES

FOR THE

BEGINNER BAKER

BITE-SIZED

FRENCH PASTRIES

FOR THE

BEGINNER BAKER

Includes Tarts, Sablés,
Madeleines *and More*

SYLVIE GRUBER

Creator of A Baking Journey

PAGE STREET
PUBLISHING CO.

Copyright © 2023 Sylvie Gruber

First published in 2023 by
Page Street Publishing Co.
27 Congress Street, Suite 105
Salem, MA 01970
www.pagestreetpublishing.com

Distributed by Macmillan, sales in Canada by The Canadian Manda Group.

27   26   25   24   23   1   2   3   4   5

ISBN-13: 978-1-64567-936-3
ISBN-10: 1-64567-936-5

Library of Congress Control Number: 2022950548

Cover and book design by Rosie Stewart for Page Street Publishing Co.
Photography by Sylvie Gruber

Printed and bound in the United States of America

TO MY GRANDMA, FRIDA,
FOR PASSING ON HER LOVE OF BEING IN THE KITCHEN.

TO MY HUSBAND, ARIEL,
FOR HIS NEVER-FAILING SUPPORT.

TO MY SON, NOAH,
WHO PUTS A SMILE ON MY FACE EVERY SINGLE DAY.

CONTENTS

INTRODUCTION

Above all, keep it simple.
—August Escoffier

Biting into a fudgy chocolate fondant cake. A bag of fresh chouquettes. The buttery crust of a tart shell. The beauty of French pastry can often be found in the simplest of things.

When I explain to people that I develop baking recipes for a living, I am often told, "Oh, I can't bake, it is too complicated and takes too much time!" This book was written with that in mind, because with a few simple techniques, quality ingredients and the curiosity to try out new things, you can create the most amazing, uncomplicated desserts!

In this book, I've decided to focus on small, easy and delicious (should I say *gourmand*?) bites and treats. The kind of baked goods you can enjoy during afternoon tea (*le goûter* in French), have on the go or even serve for dessert. These are simple, nostalgic recipes that will let you travel to France from the convenience of your kitchen.

Madeleines, sablés, moelleux cakes, financiers, crème brûlée, chocolate mousse . . . Recipes that once may have seemed out of reach or too fancy to try out can now easily be re-created in your own kitchen with basic ingredients and minimal baking utensils.

Via easy-to-follow recipes, we will also explore a wide range of fundamental techniques that can be reused and transformed to create your own desserts. After all, a classic pâte sablée (French shortcrust pastry), a basic pâte à choux (choux pastry) and a luscious crème pâtissière (pastry cream) are the perfect foundation to French pastry.

Come join me on a French baking journey, and bon appétit!

Sylvie Gruber

BASE RECIPES

A solid base is where any good recipe starts. The world of French pastry is broad and varied but always relies on simple techniques and recipes. Learn how to make a classic pastry like a Pâte Sablée (page 13) and you've got yourself a base to create many delicious tarts or even cookies. Master the Crème Pâtissière (page 16) to not only make the most delicious, creamiest custard filling ever—but also as a foundation to more complex creams such as a crème diplomate.

These traditional recipes are used throughout the book to make tarts, choux and desserts. With a simple twist, they can be turned into something more complex (but still just as easy to make) such as the chocolate crème pâtissière inside the Chocolate Choux à la Crème (page 53), the Ginger Almond Cream used in the Ginger Pear Galettes (page 40) or the milk chocolate and praliné filling in the Sablé Sandwiches (page 93).

PÂTE SABLÉE
(SHORTCRUST PASTRY)

A delicious tart always starts here: a good tart shell! This pâte sablée is not only easy to make, but it is also extremely versatile. It is firm enough to have a good crunch but still has a flaky texture. I personally always use a food processor to make this kind of pastry, but it can be made by hand, too (see Pro Tip #2). If you have never made pastry before, do not worry. With a little bit of practice, you will soon become a pâte sablée master!

MAKES 15 TO 24 TARTLETS

250 g all-purpose flour

50 g powdered sugar

¼ tsp fine salt

120 g unsalted butter, cubed and very cold

1 large egg

1. In a food processor, combine the flour, powdered sugar and salt. Pulse to mix, then add the butter. Process for 30 seconds to 1 minute, or until you get tiny crumbs of butter. The mixture should resemble thick sand.

2. Add the egg and process until a rough, slightly crumbly dough comes together. If you press some crumbs together, they should stick. If too dry, add a few drops of very cold water and mix again until you reach the desired consistency.

3. Place the dough between two sheets of parchment paper. Using a rolling pin, roll into a large disk that is about ¼ inch (4 mm) thick. Chill for 1 hour minimum or up to 24 hours. Your pâte sablée is ready to be used to create delicious tarts!

PRO TIP #1: Use a rolling pin with thickness rings or thickness band guides to roll the pastry at an even thickness.

PRO TIP #2: If you don't have a food processor, the pastry can be made by hand (or with the help of a pastry blender) by rubbing the cold butter into the dry ingredients until you get very small crumbs. In a small bowl, whisk the egg, add to the crumbs, then gently knead until you get a smooth dough. Roll out, then chill for at least 2 hours before using.

PÂTE À CHOUX
(CHOUX PASTRY)

Pâte à choux is a pastry that does require a bit of practice to master. But, trust me, the learning process is worth it! With this pastry, you can make choux buns, éclairs, profiteroles, cruller donuts, churros and other delicious treats. Pâte à choux can be made with either milk or water, or a combination of both. I personally like to use only water to get a crunchier texture. For slightly softer but richer choux, the water can be replaced with whole milk. For a good combination of texture and flavors, you can use half water and half milk.

MAKES 15 TO 20 CHOUX BUNS

125 ml water

5 g superfine or granulated sugar

Pinch of fine table salt

50 g unsalted butter

75 g all-purpose flour, sifted

2 large eggs, at room temperature

1. In a small saucepan, combine the water, sugar, salt and butter. Heat over medium heat until the butter has melted and the mixture starts to simmer. Remove from the heat and add the flour all at once. Use a stiff spatula or wooden spoon to mix until you get a thick paste (called a *panade*). Place the saucepan back over medium heat and cook for 2 minutes while continuously stirring the panade and pressing it against the sides and bottom of the saucepan to dry it out. You should see a thin film form at the bottom of the saucepan. Transfer the panade to a large, clean bowl or the bowl of a stand mixer fitted with the paddle attachment, and let cool for 5 to 10 minutes, or until it doesn't feel hot to the touch.

2. In a small bowl, whisk the eggs until the whites and yolks are well combined. Pour the whisked eggs into the panade about 1 tablespoon (15 ml) at a time and mix well with a stiff spatula or wooden spoon, or the paddle attachment of a stand mixer. The mixture seems to split at first, but it comes back together after being well stirred. Mix in more egg until you get the desired consistency—even if you have some egg left (see Pro Tip). How to know when to stop adding more egg? The pastry should be smooth, shiny and supple. Also, when you pick up some of the pastry with the spatula, it should fall back slowly and the leftover hanging pastry should form a "V" shape.

3. The pâte à choux can be used immediately or be stored in the fridge for up to 24 hours, covered with plastic wrap that is touching its surface to prevent any air pockets. Allow the pastry to come back to room temperature before using it.

PRO TIP: The exact quantity of eggs can vary slightly based on different factors, such as the brand of flour, size of the eggs or how much you dried out the panade on the stove. You might need more or less than two eggs—always rely on the consistency of the pastry rather than on the recommended quantity of eggs.

CRÈME PÂTISSIÈRE
(PASTRY CREAM)

It doesn't get more basic—and more classic—than a vanilla crème pâtissière. This creamy, luscious custard requires only five basic ingredients. It can be used in so many different ways: to fill pastries, choux, tarts and cakes, or as a base to create more complex creams, such as crème diplomate or mousseline cream. Although the basic version is simply made with vanilla, you can also flavor crème pâtissière with chocolate (such as for the Chocolate Choux à la Crème, page 53), fruit purees and juices, coffee or nut pastes. Butter can also be mixed into the crème pâtissière once it is cooked to create a richer cream.

MAKES ABOUT 650 G CRÈME PÂTISSIÈRE

500 ml whole milk

8 g vanilla paste, or 1 fresh vanilla bean

4 large egg yolks, at room temperature

40 g superfine or granulated sugar

40 g cornstarch

1. In a small saucepan, combine the milk and vanilla paste. Over low heat, bring to a simmer. If using a fresh vanilla bean, slice it in half, scrape out the seeds with a small knife and add it to the milk along with the leftover pod. When the milk starts to simmer, turn off the heat, cover the saucepan with a lid and let infuse for 15 to 20 minutes. Remove the pod (if using).

2. In a medium-sized heatproof bowl, whisk the egg yolks and sugar for about 2 minutes, or until lighter in color. Mix in the cornstarch, then slowly pour in the warm milk while whisking. When completely smooth, transfer the whole mixture back into the saucepan.

3. Cook over very low heat, continuously stirring, for about 5 minutes, or until the cream starts to thicken. Once the cream begins to simmer, cook for an additional 30 seconds, then remove from the heat. The cream should be thick and smooth and coat the back of a spoon. Transfer to a clean bowl or shallow container, cover with plastic wrap touching the surface of the cream and refrigerate for at least 2 hours, or up to 24 hours.

PRO TIP #1: Always cook crème pâtissière over low heat to avoid overcooking the egg yolks, which would create a lumpy, curdled custard. If it does curdle, you can smooth it out with an immersion blender used on the lowest speed.

PRO TIP #2: The exact cooking time can vary, based on the specific heat of your stove and the size of the saucepan.

CRÈME D'AMANDE (ALMOND CREAM)

Crème d'amande is one of those basic French recipes that is both versatile and super easy to make. It simply combines four ingredients used at a 1:1:1:1 ratio (same weight for all the ingredients). This cream is used mostly as a baked filling for tarts but can also be baked inside croissants to make almond croissants or mixed with crème pâtissière to make frangipane cream (for a galette des rois, for example). As suggested by its name, the main ingredient here is almond meal. But you can actually replace the almond meal with other ground nuts, such as pistachios (see the Strawberry and Pistachio Tartlets, page 26), for a different flavor and texture.

MAKES 400 G CRÈME D'AMANDE

100 g unsalted butter, very soft

100 g powdered sugar, sifted

2 large eggs (equivalent to 100 g), at room temperature

100 g almond meal

1. In the bowl of a stand mixer fitted with a paddle attachment or in a large bowl if using an electric hand mixer, combine the butter and powdered sugar. Mix for 2 to 3 minutes on high speed to cream, stopping to scrape the bowl with a spatula if needed. You should get a light, fluffy paste that has increased in volume.

2. Slowly mix in the eggs until fully combined.

3. Add the almond meal and slowly mix until you get a thick paste. Use immediately or store in the fridge, covered with plastic wrap touching its surface, for up to 24 hours. Allow to soften at room temperature for 15 minutes before use, if stored in the fridge.

PRO TIP: If the mixture splits once you add the eggs, it usually means that the butter was too cold and the emulsion (a combination of two ingredients that don't usually bind, such as water and fat) failed. The mixture should come back together once you add the almond meal.

PÂTE DE PRALINÉ
(PRALINE PASTE)

This incredibly decadent paste is made from blending praliné (caramelized roasted nuts). It is traditionally made with almonds but can be prepared with a variety of nuts and seeds—or a combination of different nuts, as shown here. A classic pâte de praliné is made from the exact same quantity of nuts and sugar (50% nuts, 50% sugar), but you can play around slightly with these ratios to suit your own taste. There are many ways to use pâte de praliné, such as inside a cake batter (see my Praliné-Filled Madeleines, page 114), combined with chocolate to make ganaches or spreads (see the Praliné-Filled Sablé Sandwiches, page 93) or mixed with a cream, such as the praliné mousseline cream used to make a classic Paris-Brest.

MAKES 400 G PÂTE DE PRALINÉ

100 g hazelnuts, preferably skinned

100 g almonds, preferably skinned

200 g superfine or granulated sugar

30 ml water

⅓ tsp flaky sea salt

1 tsp vanilla paste (optional)

1. Preheat your oven to 350°F (180°C). Line a baking sheet with parchment paper or a baking mat and spread the hazelnuts and almonds on it. Roast in the oven for 10 minutes, then transfer the baking sheet to a wire rack to cool. Optionally, if using unpeeled nuts, rub inside a clean tea towel to remove the skin.

2. In a medium-sized, heavy-bottomed saucepan, combine the sugar and water and heat over medium heat. Let cook for 10 to 15 minutes without stirring or touching the sugar. When it has completely melted and the transparent sugar starts to turn light yellow, lower the heat to low and cook for a few more minutes, or until it turns light amber brown. Be careful not to overcook at this point, or the caramel will start to burn and taste bitter.

3. Pour the hot caramel over the roasted nuts on the baking sheet to fully cover them. Be careful; the caramel will be extremely hot and will burn you if touched. Let cool completely for 30 minutes to 1 hour, or until the caramel has completely hardened and can easily be broken into pieces.

4. Break the mixture into small pieces (be careful; the hardened product can be sharp) and place in a powerful food processor. Process for 2 to 3 minutes, or until you get a rough powder. This powder, called pralin, can be used in dessert preparation to add flavor and crunch. Continue to process on high speed for 15 to 20 minutes; the powder will start to turn into a thick paste as the nuts release their oil.

5. Add the salt and vanilla paste (if using) and keep on processing until you get a very smooth and fluid (but still very slightly crunchy) paste. Pâte de praliné can be stored in the fridge for weeks.

PRO TIP: You will need a very powerful food processor to get from hard nuts to a liquid paste. If the food processor starts to overheat while you blend, stop and let it cool before continuing to blend.

TARTLETS & CHOUX

It does not get more French than tarts and choux. And they are both my favorite things to bake! They are incredibly versatile in both their shape and choice of fillings and toppings.

No other recipes allow you to practice your French pastry basics as tarts do. Once you have mastered the basic tart pastry (pâte sablée), you can experiment with many, many delicious filling ideas, including a classic crème pâtissière, a crème d'amande filling or even a chocolate ganache.

If making tart pastry from scratch intimidates you, do not worry; in this chapter, you will find amazing ways to use store-bought puff pastry as well. Through some of the recipes that use puff pastry, you will also learn how to make meringue, fruit compotes and caramel.

Mastering pâte à choux does require a bit of practice, but what a reward it is to get gorgeous choux buns, festive profiteroles and little éclairs. Along with my basic go-to pâte à choux recipe, you will get to learn other pastry basics, such as Chantilly cream, hot chocolate sauce and craquelin cookie topping.

BLUEBERRY AND ALMOND TARTLETS

This recipe is a great example of how crème d'amande is used in French pastry to create a delicious soft layer inside tarts. These blueberry and almond tarts are all about textures and flavors: the crunchy pâte sablée, spongy almond filling and fresh burst of blueberries are irresistible!

MAKES 15 TO 18 TARTLETS

1 batch Pâte Sablée (page 13)

1 batch Crème d'Amande (page 19)

200 g fresh blueberries

40 g slivered almonds

1. Prepare the pâte sablée, following the instructions on page 13. Once rolled out and chilled, cut out 3½-inch (9-cm)-wide disks of pastry and gently slide them into 3-inch (7.5-cm)- wide mini tart pans. Press on the inner sides and corners to make the pastry stick to the pan and remove any air bubbles. Cut out and remove any excess pastry with a small, sharp knife and smooth out the edges with your fingers. Chill in the refrigerator for at least 2 hours, preferably overnight. Any leftover pastry can be rerolled, chilled for 1 more hour, then cut out to make more tart shells.

2. Prick the pastry with a fork, cover with small pieces of parchment paper and fill with dried rice or baking weights. Put the pastries in the freezer while you preheat your oven to 325°F (160°C). Bake for 15 minutes, then remove from the oven, place on a wire rack, remove the weights and paper and set aside to cool. Leave the oven on.

3. Prepare the crème d'amande, following the instructions on page 19.

4. Spread a little of the crème d'amande on the bottom of each pastry shell, filling to about one-third of its height. Press four or five blueberries per tart into the cream, then sprinkle with the slivered almonds.

5. Bake for about 25 minutes, or until puffed and golden. Remove from the oven and set aside to cool completely before gently sliding the tartlets out of their pans.

PRO TIP: Crunching up the pieces of parchment paper and then unfolding them prior to placing them inside the tartlet shells will help them stay inside the shells and allow for the baking weights to be distributed more evenly.

STRAWBERRY AND PISTACHIO TARTLETS

This recipe really shows how versatile a classic crème d'amande is: You can simply replace the almond meal with another ground nut—pistachios here—to create different flavors and textures. Pistachio is often paired with fresh fruits like strawberries to balance its earthy flavors.

MAKES 15 TO 18 TARTLETS

1. Prepare the pâte sablée, following the instructions on page 13. Once rolled out and chilled, cut out 3½-inch (9-cm)-wide disks of pastry and gently slide them into 3-inch (7.5-cm)-wide mini tart pans. Press on the inner sides and corners to make the pastry stick to the pan and remove any air bubbles. Cut out and remove any excess pastry with a small, sharp knife and smooth out the edges with your fingers. Chill for at least 2 hours, preferably overnight.

2. Prick the pastry with a fork, cover with small pieces of parchment and fill with dried rice or baking weights. Put the pastries in the freezer while you preheat your oven to 325°F (160°C). Bake for 15 minutes, then remove from the oven, place on a wire rack, remove the weights and paper and set aside to cool. Leave the oven on.

3. Prepare the pistachio cream: In a food processor, process the pistachios until you get a slightly coarse powder. In a medium-sized bowl, using a spatula, or in the bowl of a stand mixer fitted with the paddle attachment, cream the butter and powdered sugar for 2 to 3 minutes, or until you get a light, fluffy paste. Mix in the eggs, then the ground pistachios.

(CONTINUED)

1 batch Pâte Sablée (page 13)

PISTACHIO CREAM

120 g shelled pistachios

100 g unsalted butter, very soft

100 g powdered sugar, sifted

2 large eggs (equivalent to 100 g), at room temperature

STRAWBERRY AND PISTACHIO TARTLETS (CONTINUED)

4. Spread a little bit of pistachio cream at the bottom of each pastry shell, filling to about one-third of its height. Slice the strawberries in half lengthwise. Top each tart with one strawberry half without pressing it into the pistachio cream too much. Roughly chop the pistachios and sprinkle them around the strawberries.

5. Place back in the oven and bake for another 25 minutes, or until puffed and golden. Remove from the oven and set aside to cool completely before gently sliding the tarts out of the pans.

FOR ASSEMBLY

8 to 9 large strawberries, hulled

50 g shelled pistachios

LEMON MERINGUE TARTLETS

There's nothing more classic—and more delicious—than a lemon meringue tart. Between the buttery, crunchy pâte sablée shells, the tangy lemon cream filling and the sweet, marshmallow-y meringue, these tarts are a true crowd-pleasing treat. This recipe will show you how you can use a simple muffin pan to create tartlet shells.

MAKES 15 TO 18 TARTLETS

1 batch Pâte Sablée
(page 13)

LEMON FILLING

50 g unsalted butter

120 ml fresh lemon juice

3 large eggs, at room temperature

80 g superfine or granulated sugar

4 g lemon zest

1.   Prepare the pâte sablée, following the instructions on page 13. Once rolled out and chilled, use a fluted cookie cutter to cut out 3-inch (7.5-cm)-wide disks of pastry. Gently slide each disk into the wells of an 18-well standard muffin pan or two 12-well standard muffin pans (you may have some empty wells). Lightly press around the inner bottom circumference to make sure the pastry is touching the pan all around. Chill for at least 2 hours, preferably overnight. Prick the pastry with a fork, cover with small pieces of parchment and fill with dried rice or baking weights. Put the pastries in the freezer while you preheat your oven to 325°F (160°C). Bake for 18 minutes, then carefully remove the weights and parchment paper and bake for an additional 5 minutes. Remove from the oven, place the pan on a wire rack and let cool completely.

2.   Prepare the lemon filling: In a quart-sized microwave-safe bowl, combine the butter and lemon juice and melt together in a microwave for about 1 minute, or in a small saucepan over low heat until the butter has completely melted. Set aside to cool. In a large bowl, whisk together the eggs and sugar until just combined. Add the warm butter mixture to the egg mixture and mix until just combined. Pour the mixture back into the bowl through a fine-mesh strainer and discard any lumps. Stir in the lemon zest.

(CONTINUED)

LEMON MERINGUE TARTLETS (CONTINUED)

3. Pour the lemon filling into the cooled-down tartlet shells and bake for 8 to 10 minutes at 325°F (160°C). The filling should be still slightly jiggly. Remove from the oven and let cool at room temperature for 30 minutes, then chill in the fridge for 1 hour.

4. Prepare the meringue topping: In a large bowl, using an electric mixer, or in the bowl of a stand mixer fitted with the whisk attachment, whisk the egg whites on medium speed until they develop soft peaks. While continuing to whisk, slowly add the sugar, 1 tablespoon (13 g) at a time. When all the sugar has been incorporated, increase the speed to high and continue to whisk until stiff peaks form.

5. Place the meringue into a pastry bag fitted with a ½-inch (1.2-cm) round or star-shaped piping tip. Pipe small dollops over each lemon tart. Serve as is or (carefully) toast the meringue using a kitchen torch.

MERINGUE

2 large egg whites (equivalent to 60 g)

120 g superfine or granulated sugar

PRO TIP #1: Don't mix the lemon filling too much, as you want to avoid creating air bubbles in the mixture. Too many air bubbles will make the filling puff then collapse and crack when the tarts are baked.

PRO TIP #2: To get the best result, use a muffin pan that has a perforated bottom. This will allow for optimal air flow around the pastry and help it bake evenly.

WHITE CHOCOLATE AND RASPBERRY TARTLETS

A ganache is probably the most basic and easiest chocolate cream you can make in French pastry. It simply combines melted chocolate (white chocolate here) with a specific ratio of heavy cream. The ratio varies based on the type of chocolate used and the desired texture of the ganache. Paired with the fresh raspberries, you get tartlets that are sweet, creamy and bright in taste.

MAKES 15 TO 18 TARTLETS

1 batch Pâte Sablée
(page 13)

WHITE CHOCOLATE GANACHE

200 g white baking chocolate, chopped finely

75 ml heavy cream

FOR ASSEMBLY

150 g fresh raspberries

15–18 fresh mint leaves

1. Prepare the pâte sablée, following the instructions on page 13. Once rolled out and chilled, use a fluted cookie cutter to cut out 3-inch (7.5-cm)-wide disks of pastry. Gently slide each disk into the wells of an 18-well standard muffin pan or two 12-well standard muffin pans (you may have some empty wells). Lightly press on the bottom corners to make sure the pastry is touching the pan all around. Chill for at least 2 hours, preferably overnight. Prick the pastry with a fork and cover with small pieces of parchment filled with dried rice or baking weights. Put the pastries in the freezer while you preheat your oven to 325°F (160°C). Bake for 15 minutes, remove the weights and paper, then bake for another 12 to 15 minutes, or until fully baked and golden. Remove from the oven and set aside to cool completely.

2. Prepare the white chocolate ganache: In a quart-sized microwave-safe bowl, heat the finely chopped white chocolate in the microwave for about 1 minute, or until the chocolate just starts to soften. In the meantime, in a small saucepan, heat the cream over low heat until it starts to simmer. Pour the warm cream over the partially melted chocolate, leave for 2 minutes, then gently stir to combine until smooth and glossy.

3. Pour the warm ganache into the tartlet shells, filling them about halfway up. Press two or three raspberries (depending on their size) per tart into the white chocolate. Place in the fridge to set for at least 1 hour. Garnish with fresh mint.

MINI PEACH ROSE TARTS

This recipe is proof that tarts do not need to be complicated to be both delicious and beautiful. Here, very thin slices of peaches are used to create a little rose that is simply placed over some peach jam inside the pâte sablée shells.

MAKES 24 MINI TARTS

1 batch Pâte Sablée (page 13)

30 g peach jam or preserves

3 large peaches, ripe but not too soft

15 g superfine or granulated sugar

Powdered sugar, for dusting (optional)

1. Prepare the pâte sablée, following the instructions on page 13. Once rolled out and chilled, cut out 24 disks of pastry that are about ½ inch (1.5 cm) wider than the openings of a mini muffin pan. Gently slide each pastry into the pan and lightly press on the inner bottom and sides to remove any air bubbles. Chill for at least 2 hours, preferably overnight.

2. Preheat your oven to 325°F (160°C). Prick the pastry with a fork and bake for 12 minutes without any weights. Set aside to cool for 15 minutes.

3. Scoop about ⅓ teaspoon of peach jam into the bottom of each tart shell. Wash, pit and cut the peaches in half. Cut each half into very thin slices, using a mandoline or small, sharp knife. To make the rose pattern, roll one peach slice on itself to create a spiral. Wrap four or five more slices around the center of the rose and carefully transfer it to sit on top of the jam, lightly pressing it in to make it stick. Let the rose "petals" fall back on their own. Sprinkle a little bit of sugar on top of each peach rose.

4. Bake for 30 to 35 minutes, or until the pastry shells are lightly golden and the peach roses are soft. Remove from the oven and let cool completely in the pan on a wire rack. If you wish, dust with powdered sugar just before serving.

PRO TIP: If the peaches are too firm and the rose shape doesn't stay in place, put the peach slices in a microwave-safe bowl, cover with water and microwave for 2 to 5 minutes, or until soft. Drain and pat dry before using.

MINI FLAN PÂTISSIERS

Flans pâtissiers (Parisian flans) are one of those classic desserts you find in most bakeries in France. They are often sold by the slice, but here is a mini, bite-sized version that would be great for a party or as a small snack. The crust is simply made in a muffin pan with store-bought puff pastry.

MAKES 12 FLANS

Soft butter or neutral oil, for pan

180 ml whole milk

1 large egg, at room temperature

40 g superfine or granulated sugar

20 g cornstarch

80 ml heavy cream

8 g vanilla paste

2 sheets frozen puff pastry, thawed

1. Preheat your oven to 350°F (180°C). Lightly butter or oil a 12-well standard muffin pan.

2. In a small saucepan, bring the milk to a simmer over low heat. Meanwhile, in a heatproof bowl, whisk together the egg and sugar. Add the cornstarch, then the cream and vanilla paste. Slowly pour the warm milk over the egg mixture while whisking. When smooth, transfer the entire mixture back into the saucepan.

3. Cook over low heat, stirring constantly, for 3 to 5 minutes. When the mixture has just started to thicken, turn off the heat and set aside to cool.

4. Cut out circles from the thawed puff pastry that are about ½ inch (1.2 cm) wider than the opening of the muffin pan wells. Gently slide a pastry disk into each well and press on the inner bottom circumference to ensure the pastry is touching the pan all around. Scoop the egg mixture into each puff pastry shell, filling it about halfway.

5. Bake for about 30 minutes, or until the pastry has puffed and the top of the custard has a strong golden-brown color. Remove from the oven and let cool for 15 minutes before removing from the muffin pan. Allow to cool completely before serving.

PLUM TARTES FINES

The term *tartes fines* translates literally to "thin tarts." They are easy, simple pastries that usually combine a flat layer of puff pastry with fruits. Plums are the star of this recipe, used both to make a compote filling and as a thinly sliced topping.

MAKES 6 TARTS

1. Make the plum compote: Wash the plums, remove their pits and cut the fruit into small chunks. In a small saucepan, combine the plums with the sugar and lemon juice. Heat over medium-low heat for 10 to 15 minutes, or until the plums are very soft and most of the juices have thickened. Transfer to a clean container and let cool for 30 minutes.

2. Assemble the pastries: Preheat your oven to 350°F (180°C). Cut the thawed puff pastry into six 3 x 4¾-inch (7.5 x 12-cm) rectangles. Place on a perforated baking sheet lined with parchment paper or a perforated baking mat. Fold each edge of the puff pastry up by about ¼ inch (6 mm) and prick the center with a fork. Bake for 15 minutes, then slightly flatten the center of each pastry with the back of a fork and set aside.

3. Slice the plums in half and remove their pits. Cut each half into six thin slices. Spread some plum compote in the center of each pastry. Place six slices of plums over the compote on one side of the pastry, then another six slices on the opposite side, all facing each other toward the center of the tart.

4. Bake for 20 to 25 minutes, or until the edges of the pastries are golden and the plums are soft. Remove from the oven and let cool. When cool, dust with powdered sugar.

PLUM COMPOTE

2 fresh plums

75 g superfine or granulated sugar

15 ml fresh lemon juice

FOR ASSEMBLY

1 sheet frozen puff pastry, thawed

3 fresh plums

Powdered sugar, for dusting

PRO TIP: Do not over-fill the pastries with the plum compote, and try to keep the raised edges clear of the compote. If it leaks, it might overcaramelize and burn.

GINGER PEAR GALETTES

These galettes are a fun play on the classic tarte Bourdaloue, a tart that combines an almond cream filling with poached pears. The traditional recipe is simplified here with the use of frozen puff pastry and thinly sliced raw pears. The addition of fresh ginger in the almond cream brings a real pop of freshness and flavor.

MAKES 8 GALETTES

1. Preheat your oven to 350°F (180°C). Cut the thawed puff pastry into eight 4¾-inch (12-cm) squares. Place on a perforated baking sheet lined with parchment paper or a perforated baking mat. Using a small, sharp knife, score a ½-inch (1.2-cm) edge along the four sides of the pastry. Make sure the knife only goes about halfway through the pastry so that the edges stay attached to the center of the pastry. Prick the center of each square with a fork, then bake for 15 minutes. Remove from the oven and slightly flatten the center of each pastry with the back of a fork, leaving the edges raised. Set aside to cool completely. Lower oven temperature to 325°F (160°C).

2. Prepare the ginger almond cream filling: Follow the instructions for crème d'amande on page 19, adding the grated ginger at the same time as the eggs. Set aside.

3. Peel the pears and slice each in half. Carve out the core, then thinly slice each half lengthwise.

4. To assemble the tarts, spread an even layer of the ginger almond cream in the center of the pastries and top each tart with one-half pear's worth of sliced pear. In a small bowl, whisk together the warm melted butter with the sugar and ground ginger. Generously brush it over the pear slices.

5. Bake at 325°F (160°C) for 25 to 30 minutes, or until the cream filling is golden and the pears are slightly soft. If you wish, dust with powdered sugar before serving.

2 sheets frozen puff pastry, thawed

GINGER ALMOND CREAM
1 batch Crème d'Amande (page 19)

1 tsp grated fresh ginger

PEAR TOPPING
4 small pears, ripe but not too soft

20 g unsalted butter, melted

10 g superfine or granulated sugar

½ tsp ground ginger

TO SERVE
Powdered sugar, for dusting (optional)

APRICOT AND CRÈME PÂTISSIÈRE SQUARES

Although crème pâtissière is often used as a fresh filling topped with fruits, it can also be baked inside tarts to create a texture similar to that of a flan (see page 36). The baked custard remains creamy but with a thicker texture. Placed over flaky puff pastry and topped with a thick slice of canned apricot, this creates an easy treat perfect for breakfast or afternoon tea!

MAKES 8 PASTRIES

½ batch (about 300 g) Crème Pâtissière (page 16)

2 sheets frozen puff pastry, thawed

8 canned apricot halves in syrup, drained

1 large egg, whisked

40 g apricot jam

Powdered sugar, for dusting (optional)

1. Prepare the crème pâtissière, following the instructions on page 16. Place in an airtight container, cover with plastic wrap touching the surface and chill in the fridge for at least 1 hour.

2. Preheat your oven to 350°F (180°C). Cut the thawed puff pastry into eight 3½-inch (9-cm) squares. Place on a large perforated baking sheet lined with parchment paper or a perforated baking mat.

3. Spoon some of the chilled crème pâtissière into the center of each pastry square. Spread it around, leaving about ½ inch (1.2 cm) of the edges bare. On each square, place one canned apricot half, cut side down, on top of the crème pâtissière. Fold the four corners of each pastry square toward its center, going slightly over the apricot. Press the joints between each corner to seal the seams. Brush the puff pastry with the whisked egg.

4. Bake for 30 to 35 minutes, or until the pastry has puffed and is golden. Place the baking sheet on a wire rack to cool. While the pastries are still warm, brush each apricot with some apricot jam. If you wish, dust with powdered sugar when cool.

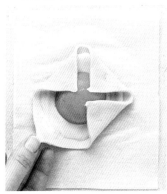

CHERRY CHAUSSONS

Chaussons are a French version of a fruit turnover or hand pie. Although they are most commonly found with an apple filling, my personal favorite has always been cherry chaussons. The cherries are cooked into a chunky compote that is used as a filling inside a triangle of puff pastry. The raw sugar sprinkled on top adds a great crunch.

MAKES 8 CHAUSSONS

1. Make the cherry compote filling: Pit the cherries, slice them in half and place in a small saucepan along with the sugar, lemon juice, water and vanilla. Cook over medium-low heat, stirring occasionally to make sure the fruits don't stick to the bottom of the pan, for 20 to 25 minutes, or until the cherries are soft and most of the juices have reduced to a thick syrup. Transfer to a clean bowl and let cool for 15 minutes.

2. Preheat your oven to 350°F (180°C). Cut the thawed puff pastry into eight 4½-inch (12-cm) squares. Arrange the squares on one or two large perforated baking sheets lined with parchment paper or a perforated baking mat.

3. Assemble the pastries: Place a little bit of the cherry compote on one-half of the puff pastry square, in a triangle taken diagonally, leaving at least a ½-inch (1.2-cm) margin on the edges all around. Brush a little bit of egg on all four edges, then fold the compote-free side of the pastry over the filling to form the pastry into a triangle. Press on the seams to make them stick, then seal the edges by pressing them together with a fork.

4. Brush the top of each pastry with the remaining egg, then cut a small opening in the shape of an X into the top of each pastry. Top with a generous sprinkle of raw sugar.

5. Bake for 30 to 35 minutes, or until puffed and golden. Remove from the oven and let cool completely before serving.

CHERRY COMPOTE FILLING

400 g pitted cherries

60 g superfine or granulated sugar

45 ml fresh lemon juice

15 ml water

1 tsp vanilla extract

FOR ASSEMBLY

2 sheets frozen puff pastry, thawed

1 large egg, whisked

30 g raw or coarse sugar

PRO TIP: Avoid over-filling the pastries and make sure to seal each side tightly, or else the compote might escape during the baking and burn.

INDIVIDUAL APPLE TARTES TATIN

These apple tartes Tatin might be a bit of a labor of love—but that labor is so worth it! Similarly to the preparation of the classic larger tart, here you need to make a caramel to fill the wells of a muffin pan then separately caramelize apples in a saucepan. There is nothing more fun than flipping the pan over when the tarts are baked, to reveal the shiny, irresistible caramelized apples.

MAKES 12 TARTS

....

1. Prepare the caramel: In a small saucepan, stir together the sugar, water and lemon juice. Heat over medium-low heat. Without touching the sugar at all, let cook for 10 to 15 minutes, or until it becomes a light amber color. Remove from the heat and carefully whisk in the butter and salt until completely smooth. Immediately, evenly pour the caramel into the wells of a 12-well muffin pan, coating only the bottom of the wells. If the caramel hardens too quickly to pour, place back on the heat for a few seconds. Set the muffin pan aside.

2. Peel the apples, cut them in half and remove the core. In a very large skillet, combine the butter, sugar, water and lemon juice. Heat over medium-low heat. When the butter has melted, place the apple halves, cut side down, in a single layer in the pan and cover with a lid, or use aluminum foil if you don't have a lid. Cook for about 20 minutes, flipping the apples every 5 minutes. Once the apples have softened slightly and the liquid has begun to turn into a slightly thicker syrup, remove the lid. Cook for another 10 to 15 minutes, or until the liquid turns into a thick, golden syrup and the apples start to get very lightly caramelized.

(CONTINUED)

CARAMEL

100 g superfine or granulated sugar

20 ml water

30 ml fresh lemon juice

30 g unsalted butter, at room temperature

Generous pinch of fine table salt

APPLES

6 small apples

30 g unsalted butter

150 g superfine or granulated sugar

240 ml water

45 ml fresh lemon juice

INDIVIDUAL APPLE
TARTES TATIN (CONTINUED)

3. Preheat your oven to 350°F (180°C). Place one apple half, cut side facing up, in each muffin pan well on top of the set layer of caramel. Gently press to push the apple down. If too large, cut off a bit of the apple to make it fit. Top with any remaining caramel from the skillet.

4. Assemble the pastries: Cut the thawed puff pastry into disks that are slightly smaller than the muffin pan wells. Place a disk of puff pastry over each apple and press down the edges to make sure each apple is fully covered.

5. Bake for 20 to 25 minutes, or until the puff pastry is golden. Remove from the oven and let cool for 3 minutes. Run a small, blunt knife around each tart to ensure the caramel does not stick to the pan. Place a large cutting board over the muffin pan and carefully flip it over to release the tartes Tatin. Serve warm.

FOR ASSEMBLY
2 sheets frozen puff pastry, thawed

CHANTILLY CHOUX AU CRAQUELIN

Making a craquelin cookie topping is a very simple way to upgrade a classic choux pastry. Not only does it add a lovely crunch to the baked goods, but it also helps the choux buns rise into homogeneous little balls. These choux au craquelin are filled with the easiest cream filling you can make: Chantilly cream.

MAKES 15 CHOUX

CRAQUELIN

30 g unsalted butter, very soft

30 g light brown sugar

30 g all-purpose flour

1. Prepare the craquelin: In a small bowl, mix together the butter and brown sugar with a spatula until combined. Add the flour and mix until you get a thick paste. Place the paste between two sheets of parchment paper and, using a rolling pin, very thinly roll to a thickness of about ⅟₃₂ inch (1 mm). Slip a baking sheet beneath the bottom sheet of parchment and chill the paste in the freezer for 30 minutes, or until hard.

(CONTINUED)

CHANTILLY CHOUX AU CRAQUELIN (CONTINUED)

2. Preheat your oven to 350°F (180°C) and line a large baking sheet with parchment paper. Prepare the pâte à choux, following the instructions on page 14. Transfer the pastry to a piping bag fitted with a ¾-inch (2-cm) round piping tip. Holding the pastry bag perpendicular to the baking sheet, pipe small mounds of pastry that are about 1½ inch (4 cm) wide and ¾ inch (2 cm) tall, leaving space between the mounds as they will expand in the oven. Take the craquelin out of the freezer and remove the top sheet of parchment paper. Using a cookie cutter that is approximately the same width as the choux buns, cut out small disks of craquelin. Gently lift each disk using a small offset spatula, and place one on top of each choux pastry. If the craquelin gets soft, place back in the freezer for a few minutes.

3. Bake for 30 minutes, or until the choux buns have nicely puffed and the craquelin looks golden (do not open the oven door while the choux bake). Turn off the oven, slightly open the oven door, use a wooden spoon to keep it open and leave like that for 15 minutes. Take the baking sheet out of the oven and place the baking sheet on a wire rack and allow to cool completely.

4. Prepare the Chantilly cream: In a large bowl, using an electric hand mixer, or in the bowl of a stand mixer fitted with the whisk attachment, combine the cream, powdered sugar and vanilla paste. Start whisking on medium speed, slowly increasing to high speed until you get stiff peaks. Transfer the Chantilly cream to a pastry bag fitted with a ½-inch (1.2-cm) star tip.

5. When completely cool, slice each choux bun in half. Fill the bottom halves of the choux with the cream filling, then continue to pipe more filling on top in a circular motion. Place the choux tops over the cream.

1 batch Pâte à Choux (page 14)

CHANTILLY CREAM

400 ml heavy whipping cream (at least 30% fat content), cold

30 g powdered sugar, sifted

1½ tsp vanilla paste

> **PRO TIP:** To create a Chantilly cream that is more stable, you can replace one-third to half of the heavy cream with mascarpone.

CHOCOLATE CHOUX À LA CRÈME

Choux à la crème are delicious little choux buns with cream filling. The most classic choux à la crème are filled with a simple vanilla crème pâtissière or Chantilly cream—but my favorite way to serve them is with a luscious chocolate filling.

MAKES 15 CHOUX

1. Prepare the chocolate pastry cream: In a medium-sized saucepan, heat the milk over low heat until it starts to simmer. In the meantime, in a heatproof bowl, whisk together the egg yolks and sugar, then mix in the cornstarch. Slowly pour the warm milk over the egg mixture while whisking. When smooth, transfer it all back into the saucepan. Cook over low heat for about 5 minutes while stirring constantly. When it has thickened, remove from the heat, add the chocolate and stir until completely melted. Transfer to a large, clean bowl and top with plastic wrap touching the surface of the pastry cream. Chill in the fridge for 2 hours.

2. Preheat your oven to 350°F (180°C) and line a large baking sheet with parchment paper. Prepare the pâte à choux, following the instructions on page 14. Place the pastry in a piping bag fitted with a ¾-inch (2-cm) round piping tip. Holding the pastry bag perpendicular to the prepared baking sheet, pipe small mounds that are about 1½ inches (4 cm) wide and ¾ inch (2 cm) tall, leaving space between the mounds.

3. Bake for 30 minutes, or until the choux buns have nicely puffed and their tops look golden (do not open the oven door while the choux bake). Turn off the oven, slightly open the oven door, use a wooden spoon to keep it open and leave like that for 15 minutes. Take the baking sheet out of the oven and place the baking sheet on a wire rack and allow to cool completely.

4. Place the chocolate cream in a piping bag fitted with a ¼-inch (6-mm) round piping tip. Poke a small hole at the bottom of each choux bun with a knife, then fill with the cream. Serve immediately.

CHOCOLATE PASTRY CREAM

500 ml whole milk

4 large egg yolks, at room temperature

40 g superfine or granulated sugar

25 g cornstarch

120 g dark baking chocolate, chopped finely

FOR ASSEMBLY

1 batch Pâte à Choux (page 14)

PRO TIP: To get a super smooth chocolate pastry cream, use an immersion blender to mix the softened chocolate into the pastry cream.

CHOUQUETTES

There is something magical about chouquettes—they always disappear as soon as they come out of the oven! These little choux buns, topped simply with crispy pearl sugar, are often sold by the bag in bakeries in France for morning or afternoon tea. You can serve them plain or fill them with cream.

1 batch Pâte à Choux (page 14)

60 g pearl sugar

MAKES 18 TO 20 CHOUQUETTES

1. Preheat your oven to 350°F (180°C) and line a large baking sheet with parchment paper. Prepare the pâte à choux, following the instructions on page 14. Transfer the pastry to a piping bag fitted with a ½-inch (1.2-cm) round piping tip.

2. Holding the pastry bag perpendicular to the prepared baking sheet, pipe small mounds of pastry that are about 1¼ inches (3 cm) wide and ½ inch (1 cm) tall. Leave some space between the choux buns, as they will expand in the oven.

3. Generously top each choux bun with pearl sugar. Gently shake the baking sheet back and forth to make all the extra pearl sugar crystals stick to the side of the choux buns.

4. Bake for 25 minutes, or until the choux buns have nicely puffed and their tops look golden (do not open the oven door while the choux are baking). Turn off the oven, slightly open the oven door, use a wooden spoon to keep it open and leave like that for 15 minutes. Take the baking sheet out of the oven and place it on a wire rack and allow to cool completely.

PRO TIP: You can make your own pearl sugar by finely crushing some white sugar cubes.

STRAWBERRY ICE CREAM PROFITEROLES

When you order profiteroles at a restaurant in France, don't expect to receive cream puffs. You will get choux buns filled with ice cream and topped with a warm chocolate sauce! It is one of the desserts that is most often made for special occasions at my parents' house—and is always a hit!

MAKES 15 PROFITEROLES

1 batch Pâte à Choux (page 14)

120 g dark baking chocolate

80 ml whole milk

1 L strawberry ice cream

1. Preheat your oven to 350°F (180°C) and line a large baking sheet with parchment paper. Prepare the pâte à choux, following the instructions on page 14. Place the pastry in a piping bag fitted with a ½-inch (1.2-cm) round piping tip.

2. Holding the pastry bag perpendicular to the prepared baking sheet, pipe small mounds of pastry that are about 1½ inches (4 cm) wide and ¾ inch (2 cm) tall. Leave some space between the choux buns, as they will expand in the oven. With a damp finger, slightly smooth out the top of the choux buns, if needed.

3. Bake for 30 minutes, or until the choux buns have nicely puffed and their tops look golden (do not open the oven door while the choux bake). Turn off the oven, slightly open the oven door, use a wooden spoon to keep it open and leave like that for 15 minutes. Take the baking sheet out of the oven and place it on a wire rack and allow to cool completely.

4. Finely chop the chocolate and place it in a microwave-safe bowl. Melt in a microwave for 30 seconds to 1 minute, or until the chocolate begins to turn slightly soft. In a small saucepan over low heat, heat the milk until it simmers, then pour over the chocolate. Gently stir until the chocolate is completely melted, to get a smooth sauce.

5. To serve, slice each choux bun in half. Place a scoop of strawberry ice cream on the bottom half and top with the top half. Pour the warm chocolate sauce over each choux pastry and serve immediately.

PRO TIP: To add some crunch, roast some slivered almonds in a 350°F (180°C) oven for 10 minutes and sprinkle them over the chocolate sauce.

MINI VANILLA ÉCLAIRS

Another great French bakery classic, éclairs are an elongated version of choux buns filled with a cream and topped with a glaze. This recipe is a simple take on the most classic of all éclairs.

MAKES 15 ÉCLAIRS

1. Prepare the vanilla crème pâtissière, following the instructions on page 16. Once cooked, transfer to a clean container or bowl and cover with plastic wrap touching the surface of the cream. Chill in the fridge for 2 hours.

2. Preheat your oven to 350°F (180°C) and line a large baking sheet with parchment paper. Prepare the pâte à choux, following the instructions on page 14. Place the pastry in a piping bag fitted with a ½-inch (1.2-cm) open star or French star piping tip. Holding the pastry bag at a 45-degree angle, pipe small logs that are about 3 inches (7.5 cm) long, leaving some room between each éclair as they will expand in the oven.

3. Bake for 25 minutes, or until the éclairs have nicely puffed and their tops look golden (do not open the oven door while the choux bake). Turn off the oven, slightly open the oven door, use a wooden spoon to keep it open and leave like that for 15 minutes. Take the baking sheet out of the oven and place it on a wire rack and allow to cool completely.

4. Remove the pastry cream from the fridge and whisk to loosen it. Transfer to a pastry bag fitted with a ³⁄₁₆-inch (4-mm) round piping tip. With a small knife, poke two holes at the bottom of the éclairs, one on each side. Press the piping tip inside each hole and fill the éclairs with the pastry cream. Set aside.

5. Make the chocolate glaze: In a heatproof bowl set atop a saucepan of boiling water (do not let the water touch the bowl), melt the chocolate until fully melted. Add the oil to the chocolate and stir until smooth and shiny. Dip the top of each éclair in the chocolate and shake gently to remove any excess chocolate. Place on a flat tray or plate, then chill in the fridge to set for 30 minutes before serving.

1 batch Crème Pâtissière (page 16)

1 batch Pâte à Choux (page 14)

CHOCOLATE GLAZE

120 g dark baking chocolate, chopped finely

15 ml neutral oil, such as canola

PRO TIP: You will know the éclairs are filled with cream once some of the filling starts to come out of the first hole while you are piping into the second hole.

PETITS GÂTEAUX

When someone says "French pastry," cakes might not be what first pops into your mind. But French cuisine is packed with many amazing cakes! You might not often see them in bakeries, but you will definitely find families making them at home on a Sunday afternoon.

These types of simple, easy cakes, such as Quatre-Quart Loaves (page 67), are called *gâteaux de grand-mère*, meaning "grandmother's cakes," which refer to those traditional family recipes passed down from generation to generation.

Other cakes, such as the Chocolate and Orange Marbled Cakes (page 64) or Mini Pain d'Épices (page 71), are referred to as *gâteaux de voyage*, or "travel cakes"—simply because they are easy to transport and last for a while at room temperature.

And let's not forget moelleux, a type of cake that uses whipped egg whites for rising and a light, fluffy texture. Although its most common version is made with chocolate, you can make a moelleux cake with a wide variety of fruits and nuts.

COFFEE CANELÉS

Another personal favorite, canelés are a pastry that cannot be mistaken for another. They are made in special fluted pans (traditionally copper molds lined with melted beeswax) and baked at a high temperature for a long time to create the most incredible mix of textures. The exterior is caramelized and crunchy while the center is soft and custardy. The basic version is flavored with vanilla and rum, but I created a breakfast version that is made with coffee.

MAKES 12 CANELÉS

500 ml whole milk

50 g unsalted butter, plus more for pan

8 g instant coffee granules

2 large eggs

2 large egg yolks

150 g superfine sugar

130 g all-purpose flour

⅓ tsp fine table salt

45 ml rum

1. In a small saucepan, combine the milk, butter and instant coffee granules. Stir, then place over low heat. When all the butter has melted and the milk starts to simmer, remove from the heat and set aside.

2. In a large bowl, whisk together the eggs, egg yolks and superfine sugar. Mix in the flour and salt. Pour in the warm milk mixture while stirring. Add the rum, then mix well until you get a very smooth, liquid batter. Transfer to an airtight container and refrigerate for 12 to 24 hours. When you are ready to bake, remove from the fridge and leave at room temperature for 1 hour. Gently stir with a spatula to remix all the ingredients.

3. Preheat your oven to 420°F (215°C). Generously butter a metal canelé pan, using a pastry brush and very soft butter. Pour the batter into the prepared canelé pan, filling each mold about two-thirds full. Tap the pan on a hard surface to pop any air bubbles. Place in the oven and bake for 15 minutes, then lower the temperature to 350°F (180°C) and bake for another 40 to 45 minutes. The top of the canelés should be quite dark. Remove from the oven and let cool in the pan for 10 minutes, then carefully flip the pan over to release the canelés. Let cool for 30 minutes before serving.

PRO TIP: The traditional recipe is made in copper pans, but I find that a metal canelé pan (such as steel or aluminum) works just as well for a fraction of the price. They can be found online or in specialty stores. I do not recommend using a silicone canelé pan that will not give you the right crunchy, caramelized exterior.

CHOCOLATE AND ORANGE MARBLED CAKES

There is something so fun and mesmerizing about marbled cakes. Not knowing what pattern you are going to get when you slice through the cake is part of the fun! This version uses one of my favorite flavor combinations: chocolate and orange. For even more decadent cakes, you can drizzle them with melted chocolate.

MAKES 8 MINI CAKES

1. Preheat your oven to 350°F (180°C). Oil or butter, then flour a mini loaf pan with eight 2½ x 4-inch (6.5 x 10-cm) molds. Tip the pan upside down and tap its underside to remove any excess flour.

2. Make the orange batter: In a large bowl, whisk together the egg and sugar for 1 minute. Mix in the oil, orange juice and zest, then the flour, baking powder and salt. Mix until just combined and set aside.

3. Make the chocolate batter: In a separate large bowl, whisk together the egg and sugar for 1 minute. Mix in the oil and cream, then sift in the flour, cocoa powder, baking powder and salt. Mix until just combined.

4. Using a teaspoon, place small dollops of batter in the prepared molds of the mini loaf pan, alternating between the chocolate and orange batters. Continue to alternate layers of batter until both batters are used. Slightly swirl the two batters using a skewer or small knife, going all the way down the bottom of the pan.

5. Bake for 18 to 20 minutes, or until a skewer comes out clean. Remove from the oven and let cool completely on a wire rack before removing the cakes from the pan. If the cakes stick, run a small, blunt knife between the cakes and the pan, then gently lift them out.

Neutral oil or melted butter, for pan

ORANGE BATTER

1 large egg, at room temperature

60 g superfine or granulated sugar

60 ml canola or other neutral cooking oil

80 ml fresh orange juice

6 g orange zest (from 1 large orange)

120 g all-purpose flour, plus more for the pan

1 tsp baking powder

Pinch of fine table salt

CHOCOLATE BATTER

1 large egg, at room temperature

60 g superfine or granulated sugar

60 ml canola or other neutral cooking oil

80 ml heavy cream

75 g all-purpose flour

20 g unsweetened cocoa powder

1 tsp baking powder

Pinch of fine table salt

PRO TIP: Try not to overswirl the two cake batters, or they will start turning into one.

QUATRE-QUART LOAVES

It really doesn't get much easier than a quatre-quart! The name translates to "four quarters," in reference to the four ingredients used in the exact same quantities to make the cake. Some versions are made with whisked egg whites; others simply use baking powder. My personal preference is baking powder—for both simplicity and texture.

MAKES 8 MINI LOAVES

1. Preheat your oven to 350°F (180°C). Oil or butter, then lightly flour a mini loaf pan with 2½ x 4–inch (6.5 x 10–cm) molds. Tip the pan upside down and tap its bottom to remove any excess flour.

2. In a small, microwave-safe bowl, melt the butter in a microwave. Alternatively, melt it in a small saucepan over low heat. Remove from heat and set aside to cool.

3. In a large bowl, whisk together the eggs and sugar for 1 minute, or until slightly bubbly. Mix in the cooled melted butter and vanilla, then the flour and baking powder. Whisk slowly until smooth.

4. Pour the batter evenly into the prepared molds of the mini loaf pan and bake for about 15 minutes, or until the cakes have risen and look golden.

5. Remove from the oven and place the pan on a wire rack to cool completely before removing the loaves from the pan. Run a small, blunt knife along the edges of the pan if the cakes stick.

Neutral oil or melted butter, for pan

All-purpose flour, for dusting

150 g salted butter

3 large eggs (equivalent to 150 g without the shell), at room temperature

150 g superfine or granulated sugar

1 tsp vanilla extract

150 g all-purpose flour

1½ tsp baking powder

PRO TIP: To make the cakes in the most traditional way, start by cracking the eggs into your bowl and weighing them. Then, use the exact same weight as the eggs for the sugar, butter and flour. This recipe originates from Brittany, a region well-known for its use of salted butter, but you can use unsalted butter with a generous pinch of salt instead, if preferred.

MINI PISTACHIO AND RASPBERRY LOAVES

Grind some pistachios, add the powder to a simple yogurt-based cake and watch it transform into the prettiest, most delicious pistachio cake! These little loaves are topped with fresh raspberries that perfectly contrast with the earthy flavors and green color of pistachios.

MAKES 8 MINI LOAVES

1. Preheat your oven to 325°F (160°C). Oil or butter and then flour a mini loaf pan with 2½ x 4-inch (6.5 x 10-cm) molds. Grind the shelled pistachios in a food processor until you get a slightly coarse powder. Transfer to a medium-sized bowl and add the flour, baking powder and salt, then stir to combine and set aside.

2. In a large bowl, whisk together the sugar and eggs for about 2 minutes, or until bubbly. Mix in the oil, Greek yogurt and lemon zest, then add the pistachio mixture. Stir until just combined.

3. Pour the batter evenly into the prepared molds of the mini loaf pan. Top each loaf with three raspberry halves and a little bit of chopped pistachios.

4. Bake for 20 to 22 minutes, or until the edges are lightly golden. Remove from the oven and place the pan on a wire rack to cool completely before removing the loaves from the pan.

Neutral oil or melted butter, for pan

100 g all-purpose flour, plus more for the pan

150 g shelled pistachios

1 tsp baking powder

¼ tsp fine table salt

100 g superfine or granulated sugar

3 large eggs, at room temperature

80 ml canola or other neutral cooking oil

120 ml Greek yogurt

1 tsp lemon zest

FOR ASSEMBLY

100 g fresh raspberries, sliced in half

25 g shelled pistachios, chopped roughly

PRO TIP: When grinding the pistachios, keeping a few larger bits of nuts will provide a great texture and crunch to the cakes.

MINI PAIN D'ÉPICES

Pain d'épices is a spiced bread made with honey, traditionally served around Christmas. The specific spice combination and type of flour can differ between regions, but this quick bread is always recognizable through its deep golden color, moist crumb and amazing sweet-yet-spicy flavors.

MAKES 8 LOAVES

1. Preheat your oven to 350°F (180°C). Generously oil or butter, then flour a mini loaf pan with 2½ x 4-inch (6.5 x 10-cm) molds.

2. Make the spice mixture: In a small bowl, stir together the cinnamon, ginger, nutmeg, star anise, cloves and white pepper in a small bowl and set aside.

3. Make the honey cakes: In a small saucepan, combine the honey, milk and butter and cook over low heat until the butter has dissolved. Mix well, remove from the heat and set aside to cool.

4. In a large bowl, whisk together the egg and brown sugar for 1 minute. Mix in the honey mixture, then add the flour, spice mixture, baking soda and salt. Whisk until just combined. You should get a rather liquid batter.

5. Pour the batter evenly into the prepared molds of the mini loaf pan and bake for 18 to 20 minutes, or until puffed and golden. Remove from the oven and let cool completely in the pan on a wire rack before removing the loaves from the pan. If needed, run a small, blunt knife along the edges of the cakes before taking them out.

Neutral oil or melted butter, for pan

All-purpose flour, for dusting

SPICE MIXTURE
½ tsp ground cinnamon

½ tsp ground ginger

⅛ tsp ground nutmeg

¼ tsp ground star anise

⅛ tsp ground cloves

Pinch of ground white pepper

HONEY CAKES
250 g honey

80 ml whole milk

75 g unsalted butter

1 large egg, at room temperature

80 g dark brown sugar

175 g all-purpose flour

½ tsp baking soda

Pinch of salt

MINI APPLE CAKES

Apples are the real hero of this recipe. These super easy cakes are made with applesauce (even better if homemade) and a large quantity of apple chunks. The result is a light, fluffy little cake that is packed with melt-in-your-mouth (but still slightly crunchy) pieces of apple. This cake is traditionally made with a touch of rum, but that is optional.

MAKES 12 CAKES

1 large apple

120 g unsalted butter

2 large eggs, at room temperature

80 g light brown sugar

120 g unsweetened applesauce

175 g all-purpose flour, sifted

1½ tsp baking powder

Pinch of fine table salt

15 g raw or demerara sugar

1. Preheat your oven to 350°F (180°C). Line a 12-well standard muffin pan with paper liners. Peel, core and cut the apple into ½-inch (1.2-cm) cubes. Set aside. In a microwave-safe bowl in a microwave, or in a small saucepan over low heat, melt the butter, remove from the heat and set aside to cool.

2. In a large bowl, whisk together the eggs and brown sugar for 1 minute. Mix in the applesauce and cooled melted butter, then the flour, baking powder and salt. Stir until just combined.

3. Fold in the apple cubes with a spatula until evenly distributed in the batter. Optionally, reserve about one-quarter of the apple chunks to top the cakes. Scoop the batter into the prepared muffin pan, top each cake with the remaining apple chunks if reserved, then generously sprinkle each cake with the raw sugar.

4. Bake for 18 to 20 minutes, or until the top is golden. Remove from the oven and let cool completely in the pan on a wire rack before removing from the pan.

PRO TIP #1: Use different varieties of apples to play with the texture and flavors of the cake. For example, Granny Smith apples will give you slightly firm and tangy apple chunks. Pink Lady apples will be softer and slightly sweeter.

PRO TIP #2: If adding rum, mix in 1 tablespoon (15 ml), or to taste, with the applesauce.

MINI CHOCOLATE FONDANT CAKES

One of my favorite—and easiest—cakes, this could be called "chocolate melting cake." These mini *fondants*, whose name translates to "tender" or "melting," have the same incredibly fudgy texture and rich chocolate flavor as their larger version—and are just as easy to make, with simple ingredients. They are almost like a French version of a brownie!

MAKES 12 FONDANTS

Neutral oil or melted butter, for pan

200 g dark baking chocolate, chopped finely

150 g unsalted butter

120 g superfine sugar

4 large eggs, at room temperature

50 g all-purpose flour

¼ tsp fine table salt

1. Preheat your oven to 350°F (180°C). Grease a 12-well standard muffin pan with oil or melted butter.

2. In a heatproof bowl set atop a saucepan of boiling water (do not let the water touch the bowl), or in a microwave-safe bowl microwaving in 30-second increments and stopping to stir each time, melt the chocolate and butter until smooth. Set aside to cool.

3. In a medium-sized bowl, whisk the superfine sugar and eggs until just combined. Mix in the cooled melted chocolate mixture, then the flour and salt. Stop whisking as soon as all the ingredients are combined.

4. Scoop the batter into the prepared muffin pan, filling each muffin well about two-thirds full. Bake for 10 minutes; the center of each cake should still be soft and slightly shiny.

5. Remove from the oven and let the muffin pan cool on a wire rack for 20 minutes before lifting the cakes out of the pan.

PRO TIP: Make sure to use good-quality baking chocolate that usually comes in the form of a bar. Do not use chocolate chips, as they are designed not to melt and will give your cakes a slightly grainy texture.

PLUM AND ALMOND MOELLEUX

A moelleux is a type of cake that relies on whipped egg whites for rising and creating a soft, moist crumb—hence its name, which translates to "soft" or "fluffy." Add some almond meal to the mixture and you get yourself an incredibly moist and tasty little treat! The naturally sweet flavor of almond is perfectly balanced by the fresh, slightly tangy plums.

MAKES 12 MOELLEUX

2 plums

3 large eggs

100 g superfine sugar

120 ml canola or other neutral cooking oil

¼ tsp almond extract (optional)

100 g all-purpose flour

75 g almond meal

¼ tsp fine table salt

⅓ tsp baking powder

20 g flaked almonds

1.   Preheat your oven to 350°F (180°C). Line a 12-well standard muffin pan with paper liners. Wash and cut the plums into quarters, then cut each quarter into three slices. Set aside.

2.   Separate the egg yolks and egg whites into two separate large bowls. Set the egg yolks aside. Using a stand mixer fitted with the whisk attachment, or an electric hand mixer, whisk the egg whites on medium-high speed until they reach stiff peaks. Place in the fridge.

3.   To the bowl of egg yolks, add the superfine sugar and whisk for 1 minute, or until the mixture turns a pale beige. Mix in the oil and almond extract (if using), then the flour, almond meal, salt and baking powder. You should get a thick batter.

4.   Gently whisk about a third of the whipped egg whites into the egg yolk mixture. Switch to a silicone spatula and gently fold in the rest of the egg whites in two or three batches. Scoop the batter into the prepared muffin pan. Lightly press three slices of the plums on top of each cake and top with flaked almonds.

5.   Bake for 18 to 20 minutes, or until the cakes have risen and the edges are slightly golden. Place the pan on a wire rack to cool completely before removing the moelleux.

PRO TIP: The almond meal will make the mixture thicken quickly, so make sure to incorporate the whisked egg whites immediately. Whisking a small portion of the egg whites in first will make folding in the rest easier.

SPICED PEAR MOELLEUX

There are so many ways to customize a simple moelleux cake, such as by loading it with spices and chunks of fruits. These pear moelleux are great for fall when you are after a comforting dessert that is not too heavy. You can use any of your preferred spices to make this recipe your own.

MAKES 12 MOELLEUX

1. Preheat your oven to 350°F (180°C). Line a 12-muffin standard pan with paper liners. In a medium-sized bowl, mix together the flour, baking powder, ground cinnamon, nutmeg, ginger, allspice and salt. Set aside. Peel and core the pear and slice it into ½-inch (1.2-cm) cubes. Set aside.

2. Separate the egg yolks and egg whites, placing them in two separate large bowls. Set the egg yolks aside. Using a stand mixer fitted with the whisk attachment, or an electric hand mixer, whisk the egg whites on medium-high speed until they reach stiff peaks. Place in the fridge. To the bowl of the egg yolks, add the brown sugar and whisk for 1 minute, then add the oil and cream. Sift in the flour mixture and mix until smooth.

3. Gently whisk about a quarter of the whipped egg whites into the egg yolk mixture. Switch to a silicone spatula and gently fold in the rest of the egg whites in two or three batches. When the egg whites have been almost completely incorporated, add about half of the pear cubes and finish folding them in with the leftover egg whites.

4. Pour the batter into the prepared muffin pan and top each portion with the remaining pear chunks. Bake for 15 to 18 minutes, or until the cakes have risen and are lightly golden. Place the pan on a wire rack to cool completely before removing the moelleux.

125 g all-purpose flour

½ tsp baking powder

1 tsp ground cinnamon

¼ tsp ground nutmeg

½ tsp ground ginger

¼ tsp ground allspice

Pinch of fine table salt

1 large pear, ripe but slightly firm

3 large eggs

100 g light brown sugar

120 ml canola or other neutral cooking oil

60 ml heavy cream

SABLÉS & COOKIES

Said to have been invented in the town of Sablé-sur-Sarthe in the north-west region of France, sablés are the most popular and traditional form of French cookies. The word *sablé* also means "sandy," which perfectly fits their delicate, crumbly texture. Additionally, the sablage technique is one of the main ways to make pastry dough, whereby butter is cut into flour to create a pastry that is slightly crisp yet flaky.

French cookies can come in many shapes and forms. Each region has its own traditional specialties, such as the Sablés Bretons (page 83) in Brittany. Sablés can be compared to shortbread but tend to be richer in taste and texture, as they are usually made with a higher quantity of butter as well as eggs.

Throughout history, French pastry has often drawn influence from neighboring countries, such as Italy or Spain. Macarons and florentine cookies are some of those little treats that have crossed borders. These cookies are usually enjoyed with a cup of tea or coffee during afternoon tea.

SABLÉS BRETONS

These are possibly the most famous of all French cookies. As its name indicates, they come from the Brittany region, a region that is famous for high-quality salted butter. And using salted butter is the secret to tasty sablés bretons! Although usually turned into cookies, the dough can also be used as a base for mousse cakes or other larger desserts.

MAKES 18 COOKIES

4 large egg yolks, at room temperature, divided

75 g powdered sugar, sifted

100 g salted butter, very soft

175 g all-purpose flour

½ tsp baking powder

¼ tsp fine table salt

1. In a large bowl, using a spatula, or in the bowl of a stand mixer fitted with the paddle attachment, mix together three of the egg yolks and the powdered sugar until just smooth. Add the butter and mix to get a thick paste. Add the flour, baking powder and salt. Using a spatula, work the mixture until all the flour has been incorporated and you get a thick dough.

2. Place the dough between two sheets of parchment paper and, using a rolling pin, roll out into a large ¼-inch (6-mm)-thick disk. Place on a flat tray and chill in the refrigerator for at least 1 hour.

3. Preheat your oven to 325°F (160°C). Peel off the top sheet of parchment paper and cut out the cookies using a 2½-inch (6.5-cm)-wide fluted cookie cutter. Place the sablés on a large perforated baking sheet lined with parchment paper or a perforated baking mat.

4. In a small bowl, lightly whisk the fourth egg yolk and brush it on top of each cookie. Gently press the back of a fork over each cookie to create a crisscross pattern. Bake for 15 minutes, or until lightly golden. Remove from the oven and place the baking sheet on a wire rack to cool completely.

PRO TIP: Any leftover dough can be rerolled, chilled for another hour, then cut out to make more cookies.

DOUBLE CHOCOLATE SABLÉS

Sablés are often referred to as French shortbread but they are made with eggs. This gives the cookies a richer and more delicious melt-in-your-mouth texture. These sablés have a buttery taste and deep cocoa flavors. They are finished with a decadent (but simple) one-ingredient dark chocolate glaze.

MAKES 12 COOKIES

150 g all-purpose flour

50 g unsweetened cocoa powder

⅓ tsp fine table salt

100 g unsalted butter, soft

100 g powdered sugar, sifted

1 large egg

1 tsp vanilla extract

1. In a medium-sized bowl, mix together the flour, cocoa powder and salt, then set aside. In a separate medium-sized bowl, using an electric hand mixer, or in the bowl of a stand mixer fitted with the paddle attachment, cream the butter and powdered sugar on low speed for 2 minutes, or until the mixture turns into a smooth paste. Increase the speed to medium and mix, stopping to scrape the bowl with a spatula if needed, for 1 minute, or until soft and fluffy. Slowly mix in the egg and vanilla.

2. Sift in the flour mixture and mix on low speed for 1 to 2 minutes, or until the mixture comes together into a thick, soft and slightly sticky dough. Transfer between two sheets of parchment paper and, using a rolling pin, roll out into a ½-inch (1.2-cm)-thick disk. Place on a flat tray and refrigerate for 1 hour, or up to 24 hours.

3. Preheat your oven to 325°F (160°C). Peel off the parchment paper and cut out cookies using a 2½-inch (6.5-cm)-wide cookie cutter. Place the sablés on a large perforated baking sheet lined with parchment paper or a perforated baking mat. Leftover dough can be rerolled and chilled for 1 hour to make more cookies. Bake for 18 minutes, or until very slightly soft but dry to the touch, then remove from the oven and let the baking sheet cool completely on a wire rack.

(CONTINUED)

DOUBLE CHOCOLATE SABLÉS (CONTINUED)

4. Line a flat tray with clean parchment paper. In a heatproof bowl set atop a saucepan of boiling water (the water should not touch the bottom of the bowl), or in a microwave-safe bowl microwaving in 30-second increments, melt the chocolate. Dip half of each sablé cookie in the melted chocolate. Gently shake the cookie, then scrape its bottom against the top of the bowl to remove any excess. If the chocolate starts to harden before you finish glazing all the cookies, melt again over the saucepan or in the microwave for a few seconds.

5. Place the dipped cookies on the parchment paper and leave at room temperature for about 1 hour, or until the chocolate glaze has set.

75 g dark baking chocolate, chopped finely

PRO TIP: To roll the dough into an even layer with the right thickness, use a rolling pin with thickness rings.

BERRY-SWIRL MERINGUE COOKIES

Meringue cookies are a great way to use leftover egg whites. They have a great crispy exterior with a soft, marshmallow-y interior. Topping them with a fresh, flavorful mixed berry coulis is a simple way to balance their naturally sweet taste. Meringue cookies are super easy to make but demand patience, as they need to bake very slowly at the lowest temperature possible.

MAKES 12 MERINGUE COOKIES

1. Make the berry coulis: Slice the berries into small chunks and place in a small saucepan along with the superfine sugar and lemon juice. Cook over medium heat, stirring occasionally, for 10 to 15 minutes, or until the berries are very soft and most of the juices have thickened. Remove from the heat and let cool for 15 minutes, then blend using an immersion or regular blender to blend until smooth. Press through a fine-mesh strainer and discard any seeds. Let cool completely.

2. Make the meringues: Preheat your oven to 215°F (100°C) and line large baking sheet with parchment paper (you might need two baking sheets). In a large bowl, using an electric hand mixer, or in the bowl of a stand mixer fitted with the whisk attachment, combine the egg whites, cream of tartar and salt. Whisk on medium speed for about 3 minutes, or until they reach soft peaks. The mixture should have thickened slightly, doubled in volume and turned white. Add the sugar, 1 tablespoon (13 g) at a time while continuing to whisk. When all the sugar has been added, increase the speed to high and continue to whisk for about 2 minutes, or until the mixture has very stiff peaks. The meringue should be very thick, glossy and hold its shape well.

(CONTINUED)

BERRY COULIS
200 g mixed berries, fresh or frozen, thawed and drained

30 g superfine sugar

10 ml fresh lemon juice

MERINGUES
3 large egg whites (about 90 g)

½ tsp cream of tartar

¼ tsp salt

150 g superfine or granulated sugar

BERRY-SWIRL MERINGUE COOKIES (CONTINUED)

3. Using a medium-sized (2½-tablespoon [38-ml]) ice-cream scoop, scoop dollops of meringue onto the prepared baking sheet, leaving some room between each meringue mound. Drizzle about ½ teaspoon of the berry coulis on top of each meringue. With a skewer, gently swirl the coulis into the meringue but be careful not to deflate it. The meringue will spread out while you swirl in the coulis.

4. Bake for 2½ to 3 hours. For chewy meringues, turn off the oven when the sides are hard but the center is still very slightly soft. For crispy meringues, continue to bake until the top is hard, then turn off the oven. In either case, once the meringues are baked, leave them inside the fully closed oven to dry out for 1 hour, or until completely cool.

PRO TIP: If the meringues start to turn yellow, it is an indication that your oven is running too hot.

BUCKWHEAT SABLÉS

Sarrasin (buckwheat) is yet another traditional ingredient from the Brittany region. It is used to make buckwheat crêpes or galettes, for example. This type of flour creates an amazing deep, earthy flavor that makes these sablé cookies extra special. This recipe uses the traditional sablage mixing technique and is simply made in a few minutes with a food processor.

MAKES 18 TO 20 COOKIES

75 g all-purpose flour

100 g buckwheat flour

70 g light brown sugar

½ tsp baking powder

½ tsp flaky sea salt

90 g unsalted butter, cubed and very cold

1 large egg

1. In a food processor, combine the all-purpose flour, buckwheat flour, brown sugar, baking powder and salt. Pulse to mix. Add the butter cubes and blend until you get very small crumbs of butter. Add the egg and continue to mix until a rough, slightly sticky dough comes together.

2. Place the dough between two large sheets of parchment paper and, using a rolling pin, roll out into a large ¼-inch (4-mm)-thick disk. Chill in the fridge for at least 1 hour.

3. Preheat your oven to 325°F (160°C). Peel off the top parchment paper and cut out cookies with a 2½-inch (6.5-cm)-wide fluted cookie cutter. Place on a large perforated baking sheet lined with parchment paper or a perforated baking mat. Use the flat side of the tip of a skewer to poke two small holes in the center of each cookie. Reroll and chill leftover dough for at least 1 hour to make more cookies.

4. Bake for 13 to 15 minutes, or until the edges are very lightly golden. Remove from the oven, transfer to a wire rack and let cool completely.

PRO TIP: If you don't have a food processor, the dough can be made by hand (or with a pastry blender). Simply rub the cold butter with the dry ingredients until you get small crumbs of butter that are evenly covered by the dry ingredients. Gently knead in the egg until you get a smooth dough.

PRALINÉ-FILLED SABLÉ SANDWICHES

Even the most basic of all sablé cookies can be used to create a deliciously decadent treat such as these sandwich cookies. Two sablés are pressed around a super simple filling combining praliné paste and milk chocolate. This filling is so good, you will want to use it as a spread for breakfast or afternoon tea!

MAKES 15 TO 18 SANDWICH COOKIES

1. Prepare the sablé cookies: In the bowl of a food processor, combine the flour, powdered sugar and salt. Pulse for a few seconds to mix. Add the butter cubes and blend until you get very small crumbs. Add the egg and mix until a rough dough comes together. Transfer between two sheets of parchment paper and, using a rolling pin, roll out into a large disk that is about ¼ inch (4 mm) thick. Chill in the fridge for at least 1 hour.

2. Preheat your oven to 325°F (160°C). Peel off the top parchment paper and cut out the cookies with a 2½-inch (6.5-cm)-wide round cookie cutter. Place on a large perforated baking sheet lined with a perforated baking mat or parchment paper. Bake for 15 minutes, or until the edges get very lightly golden. Remove from the oven and transfer to a wire rack to cool completely. Reroll and chill any leftover dough for at least 1 hour to make more cookies.

3. While the sablés are cooling, prepare the filling: In a heatproof bowl set atop a saucepan of boiling water (do not let the water touch the bowl), or in a microwave-safe bowl microwaving in 30-second increments, melt the milk chocolate. When completely melted, gently mix in the pâte de praliné with a spatula. Chill for 20 minutes.

4. To assemble, pour about 1 teaspoon of the filling on the center of a sablé cookie. Top with a second cookie and gently press to spread the filling toward the edges. Chill the cookies in the refrigerator for 30 minutes, or until the filling has set, before serving.

SABLÉ COOKIES
200 g all-purpose flour

50 g powdered sugar

¼ tsp fine table salt

120 g unsalted butter, very cold and cut into small cubes

1 large egg

FILLING
75 g milk baking chocolate, chopped finely

120 g Pâte de Praliné (page 20, or store-bought)

VIENNESE SABLÉS

Viennese sablés (sometimes called spritz cookies) originally come from the Alsace region of France but are now widely popular all around the continent. This crumbly, buttery cookie is easily recognizable by its special piped "W" or round swirl. Once baked, the sablés are dipped in dark chocolate.

MAKES 12 COOKIES

180 g unsalted butter, very soft

75 g powdered sugar, sifted

1 large egg white (about 30 g)

1 tsp vanilla paste

200 g all-purpose flour, sifted

Generous pinch of fine table salt

100 g dark baking chocolate, chopped finely

1. Preheat your oven to 325°F (160°C). Line a large baking sheet with parchment paper.

2. In a large bowl, using a hand mixer, or in the bowl of a stand mixer fitted with the paddle attachment, beat the butter on medium speed for 1 minute to smooth it out, then add the powdered sugar. Mix on medium speed for 2 to 3 minutes, or until the mixture is very soft. Add the egg white and vanilla paste, and mix for another 1 to 2 minutes to get a thick, smooth paste.

3. Slowly mix in the flour and salt and stop mixing as soon as combined. Transfer the dough to a pastry bag fitted with a ½-inch (1.2-cm)-wide open star piping tip. Pipe the dough into a "W" shape on the prepared baking sheet. The cookies should be about 1½ x 3 inches (4 x 7.5 cm).

4. Bake for 12 to 14 minutes, or until the edges are slightly golden. Remove from the oven and transfer to a wire rack to cool completely. Let the prepared baking sheet cool, as you will need it for the next step.

5. In a heatproof bowl set atop a saucepan of boiling water (do not let the water touch the bowl), or in a microwave-safe bowl microwaving in 30-second increments, melt the chocolate. Dip half of each cooled cookie in the chocolate, gently shake to remove any excess and place back on the prepared baking sheet. Place in the fridge to chill for 30 minutes, or until the chocolate has set.

PRO TIP: Make sure the butter is as soft as possible (without it having melted), or the dough will be too stiff and hard to pipe. If too hard to pipe, leave at room temperature for a few minutes to allow it to soften.

COCONUT ROCHERS

These easy-to-make little treats, whose name means "coconut rocks," require only four ingredients. They are made in a way that is relatively similar to making macaroons, but it is their pyramid shapes that make them stand out. As they bake, the coconut on the exterior becomes slightly toasted and crunchy, while the center remains soft and moist.

MAKES 12 ROCHERS

75 g powdered sugar, sifted

125 g fine desiccated coconut

3 large egg whites

⅓ tsp fine table salt

1. Preheat your oven to 395°F (200°C). Line a large baking sheet with parchment paper or a baking mat.

2. In a small bowl, combine the powdered sugar and coconut. In a very clean large bowl, whisk together the egg whites and salt until the egg whites reach soft peaks (soft shaving-cream consistency). Gently stir in the coconut with a spatula until loosely mixed and slightly sticky.

3. Using a 1½-tablespoon (23-ml) ice-cream scoop, scoop small balls onto the prepared baking sheet. Gently press and mold the top of the balls with your fingers to create a pyramid shape. If the mixture sticks to your fingers, lightly wet them with water. Make sure the pyramids are packed tightly or they might break.

4. Bake for 10 to 12 minutes, or until the top is golden. Remove from the oven and let cool completely before removing from the baking sheet.

ALMOND TUILES

These golden, crispy cookies take their name from the roof tiles (*tuiles*) they resemble. A super thin cookie batter is spread over a baking sheet, then covered with crunchy flaked almonds. It is custom to give them a curved shape by placing them over a rolling pin when they have just come out of the oven and are still soft.

MAKES 18 TUILES

30 g unsalted butter

2 large egg whites

80 g superfine or granulated sugar

25 g all-purpose flour

¼ tsp fine table salt

75 g flaked almonds

1. Preheat your oven to 350°F (180°C). Line two large baking sheets (the tuiles will spread a lot) with silicone baking mats or parchment paper.

2. In a small saucepan over low heat or in a microwave-safe bowl in a microwave, melt the butter, then set aside to cool. In a large bowl, lightly whisk the egg whites and sugar for a few seconds. Add the cooled butter, then the flour and salt. Mix to get a thin, fluid batter.

3. Pour 1½ teaspoons (about 8 ml) of batter per tuile onto one of the two prepared baking sheets, leaving about 5 inches (12.5 cm) clear around each dollop of batter. With the back of a spoon, gently spread each portion of batter into a paper-thin disk that is about 3 inches (7.5 cm) wide. Generously sprinkle the flaked almonds over each cookie. Bake for 8 to 10 minutes, or until golden and crispy.

4. As soon as removed from the oven and while still hot, gently lift each tuile with a small offset spatula and place it on top of a rolling pin to give it a curved shape. They will harden very quickly.

PRO TIP: The batter should be spread out as thinly as possible to get a nice crispy texture. It should be almost translucent once spread out. The tuiles will spread out more easily on a silicone baking mat than on parchment paper.

APRICOT FLORENTINES

Classic florentines are made with sour cream and honey, which gives the flourless cookies a well-balanced sweet taste. Traditionally, florentines are made with candied fruits (usually oranges), which I have here simply replaced with a combination of dried apricots and orange zest.

MAKES 12 FLORENTINES

1. Preheat your oven to 350°F (180°C). In a medium-sized bowl, stir together the apricots, flaked almonds and orange zest. Set aside.

2. In a medium-sized saucepan, combine the sour cream, honey, sugar and salt and bring to a simmer over medium-low heat. Cook, stirring occasionally with a heatproof spatula to make sure the bottom does not burn, for about 5 minutes, or until the mixture thickens slightly. Remove from the heat.

3. Add the apricot mixture and stir well until completely coated, thick and slightly sticky. Using two spoons, carefully transfer the mixture into a 12-well standard-sized silicone muffin pan, packing about 2 tablespoons (30 ml) of the mixture per muffin well. If you don't have a silicone pan, you can place dollops of the mixture directly on a parchment-lined baking sheet, but the florentines will spread out and be thinner.

4. Bake for 15 to 18 minutes, or until the top is lightly golden. Remove from the oven and let cool completely in the pan on a wire rack before removing from the pan. The florentines will appear very soft when they come out of the oven, but will harden as they cool.

5. In a heatproof bowl set atop a saucepan of boiling water (do not let the water touch the bowl), melt the chocolate. Dip the bottom of the cooled cookies into the melted chocolate, lightly shake to remove any excess and place on a flat tray lined with parchment paper. Leave at room temperature for about 1 hour, or until the chocolate has completely set. For chewy, soft cookies, store at room temperature. For crunchy cookies, keep in the fridge.

80 g dried apricots, chopped finely

175 g flaked almonds

12 g orange zest (from 1 large orange)

120 g sour cream

45 g honey

120 g superfine or granulated sugar

½ tsp flaky sea salt

100 g dark baking chocolate, chopped finely

PRO TIP: Be careful not to overcook the sugar mixture, or it will become hard and very sticky. Use a candy thermometer if you have one: The caramel is cooked when around 245°F (118°C).

CHOCOLATE MENDIANTS

These little chocolate disks topped with an array of nuts and dried fruits are a confectionary you will often see sold in bakeries in small plastic bags. *Mendiant* translates to "beggar," in reference to Catholic monks who have taken a vow of poverty. Traditionally, the four colors of the nuts and dried fruits used as toppings (almond, hazelnut, dried figs and raisins) represent the specific Catholic orders these "beggars" belonged to. Any of your favorite dried fruits, seeds and nuts can be used here.

MAKES 20 MENDIANTS

200 g dark baking chocolate, 70% cacao, chopped finely

40 g cashews

25 g raisins

25 g shelled pistachios

30 g dried apricots, chopped finely

1. Line a large, flat tray with parchment paper. In a heatproof bowl set atop a saucepan of boiling water (do not let the water touch the bowl), or in a microwave-safe bowl microwaving in 30-second increments, melt the chocolate until completely smooth.

2. Pour small dollops, about 1½ teaspoons (8 ml) each, of the melted chocolate onto the prepared tray. Using the back of the spoon, slightly spread each mound into a 2½-inch (6.5-cm) disk. Melt again if the chocolate starts to set before you have used it all.

3. While the chocolate is still warm, top each disk with a cashew, some raisins, pistachios and small chunks of dried apricot.

4. Place in the fridge to chill for 1 hour, or until the chocolate has set.

PRO TIP: You will get the best results by using couverture chocolate, the type of chocolate that is used to make bonbons and other sweets. This is a good recipe to practice tempering chocolate with, which will give your mendiants a shiny look and a consistency that will not melt under your fingers.

MADELEINES & FINANCIERS

Madeleines were the first French pastry recipe I learned how to make. To this day, I consider them to be my real introduction to pastry and where my passion started to blossom. My own *madeleine de Proust*.

These delicate little cakes have a distinctive shape that makes them almost too pretty to eat . . . almost. The buttery taste and soft texture of a classic madeleine simply makes them impossible to resist. I cannot think of better treats to make for a fancy tea party, special occasion or dessert buffet. All it takes is a pinch of citrus zest, some spices or cocoa powder to turn them into a truly magical treat.

I discovered financiers later on in life, but they have had my heart ever since. They are my go-to recipe when I have leftover egg whites (which I often have!). These cakes have an incredibly soft and moist texture with a deliciously rich and nutty flavor, thanks to the use of ground almonds and brown butter.

Financiers have that magical characteristic of remaining fresh for days—and even improving with time! Although they're tasty enough to be enjoyed plain, you can also top them with fresh fruits, fill them with chocolate or even replace the almonds with another ground nut, as I did for my Orange Hazelnut Financiers recipe (page 122). The flavoring options are endless—and all equally delicious!

BASIC MADELEINES

Madeleines are some of the most recognizable little French cakes. With their pretty scallop shape and soft, fluffy crumb, they are always a crowd favorite. The madeleine mixture is called a *génoise*, a type of batter made when eggs and sugar are whisked together for a long time to create lots of tiny air bubbles. These tiny bubbles make the madeleines rise in the oven and create a super airy, spongy texture. In their classic form, madeleines are usually flavored by lemon zest, honey, vanilla or browning the butter .

MAKES 12 MADELEINES

50 g unsalted butter, plus soft butter for pan

1 large egg, at room temperature

35 g superfine sugar

20 ml whole milk

½ tsp vanilla extract

60 g all-purpose flour

1 tsp baking powder

Pinch of fine table salt

1. In a small, microwave-safe bowl, melt the butter in a microwave. Alternatively, melt it in a small saucepan over low heat. Set aside to cool. In a large bowl, combine the egg and superfine sugar. Whisk together for 3 to 4 minutes; the mixture should have almost doubled in volume, and look paler and thicker. Mix in the milk and vanilla. Add the flour, baking powder and salt, then mix until smooth. Lastly, add the cooled melted butter and whisk until you get a smooth, thick batter. Cover the bowl with plastic wrap touching the surface of the batter and refrigerate for at least 3 hours, preferably overnight.

2. Generously butter a metal madeleine pan with soft butter. Transfer the batter to a piping bag and cut the tip to create a small opening. Pipe the batter into the prepared pan, filling each mold no more than half full. Alternatively, simply scoop small dollops of batter into the prepared pan. It is better to bake a second batch separately rather than to overfill the pan.

3. Place the filled madeleine pan in the fridge and preheat your oven to 390°F (200°C). Bake for 3 minutes, lower the temperature to 350°F (180°C) and bake for an additional 6 minutes. The edges should be lightly golden and the center should have risen into a tall bump. Remove from the oven and let cool completely in the pan on a wire rack before removing from the pan.

*See image on page 104.

PRO TIP: Temperature is key to get the recognizable "bump" on the madeleines. It is the temperature shock between the very cold batter and the very hot oven that makes the sides of the madeleines cook quickly without too much rise while allowing for the middle to keep rising.

WHITE CHOCOLATE AND LIME MADELEINES

This recipe shows you how to easily take a basic madeleine to the next level by flavoring the batter with lime juice and zest. The white chocolate glaze provides a delicious contrast of flavor.

MAKES 12 MADELEINES

1. Make the madeleines: In a small, microwave-safe bowl, melt the butter in a microwave. Alternatively, melt it in a small saucepan over low heat. Set aside to cool. In a large bowl, combine the egg and sugar. Whisk together for 3 to 4 minutes; the mixture should have almost doubled in volume, and look paler and thicker. Mix in the lime juice and zest, then add the flour, baking powder and salt. Add the cooled melted butter and whisk until you get a smooth, thick batter. Cover the bowl with plastic wrap touching the surface of the batter and refrigerate for at least 3 hours, preferably overnight.

2. Generously butter a metal madeleine pan with soft butter. Pour the batter into a piping bag and cut the tip to create a small opening. Pipe the batter into the prepared pan, filling each mold no more than half full. Alternatively, simply scoop small dollops of batter into the prepared pan. It is better to bake a second batch separately rather than to overfill the pan.

3. Place the filled madeleine pan in the fridge and preheat your oven to 390°F (200°C). Bake for 3 minutes, lower the temperature to 350°F (180°C) and bake for an additional 6 minutes. The edges should be lightly golden and the center should have risen into a tall bump. Remove from the oven and let cool completely in the pan on a wire rack before removing from the pan.

4. Make the glaze: In a heatproof bowl set atop a saucepan of boiling water (do not let the water touch the bowl), melt the white chocolate. When smooth, gently stir in the lime juice; the chocolate should thicken. Dip one side of each madeleine in the melted chocolate and gently shake to remove any excess, then place on a flat tray and top with lime zest.

LIME MADELEINES

50 g unsalted butter, plus soft butter for pan

1 large egg

40 g superfine or granulated sugar

25 ml fresh lime juice

1 tsp lime zest (from about 1 large lime)

60 g all-purpose flour

1 tsp baking powder

Pinch of fine table salt

WHITE CHOCOLATE LIME GLAZE

60 g white baking chocolate, chopped finely

15 ml fresh lime juice

Lime zest, for garnish

ESPRESSO MADELEINES WITH CHOCOLATE SHELL

Another great way to elevate a madeleine is to create a thin, crispy and decadent chocolate shell on its bottom. And what is a better flavor combination than coffee and dark chocolate? Instead of simply dipping the espresso madeleines in chocolate, the madeleine pan itself is used as a mold to give the shell a well-defined shape.

MAKES 12 MADELEINES

....

1. Make the madeleines: In a small saucepan, heat the butter and milk over low heat. Once the butter has melted, mix in the instant espresso until fully dissolved, remove from the heat and set aside to cool. In a large bowl, combine the egg and sugar. Whisk together for 3 to 4 minutes; the mixture should have almost doubled in volume, and look paler and thicker. Add the cooled espresso mixture, then the flour, baking powder and salt. Mix until smooth, cover the bowl with plastic wrap touching the surface of the batter and refrigerate for at least 3 hours, preferably overnight.

2. Generously butter a metal or silicone madeleine pan with soft butter. Transfer the batter to a piping bag and cut the tip to create a small opening. Pipe the batter into the prepared pan, filling each mold no more than half full. Alternatively, simply scoop small dollops of batter into the prepared pan. It is better to bake a second batch separately rather than to overfill the pan.

3. Place the filled madeleine pan in the fridge and preheat your oven to 390°F (200°C). Bake for 3 minutes, lower the temperature to 350°F (180°C) and bake for an additional 6 minutes. The edges should be lightly golden and the center should have risen into a tall bump. Remove from the oven and let cool completely in the pan before removing from the pan.

ESPRESSO MADELEINES

50 g unsalted butter, plus soft butter for pan

40 ml whole milk

6 g instant espresso powder or granules

1 large egg, at room temperature

45 g superfine or granulated sugar

80 g all-purpose flour

1 tsp baking powder

Pinch of fine table salt

4. Clean the empty madeleine pan and let it fully dry. In a heatproof bowl set atop a saucepan of boiling water (do not let the water touch the bowl), or in a microwave-safe bowl microwaving in 30-second increments, melt the chocolate until completely smooth. Mix in the instant coffee until fully dissolved. Pour about 1 teaspoon of chocolate inside each madeleine mold and spread it slightly with the back of a spoon. Place each madeleine into a chocolate-coated mold and gently press to spread the chocolate; you should see the chocolate come up the sides of the madeleine. Place in the fridge for 30 minutes, then in the freezer for 15 minutes to fully set the shell. Very gently lift the madeleines out of the pan.

CHOCOLATE SHELL

75 g dark baking chocolate, chopped finely

1 tsp instant espresso powder or granules

PRO TIP: For this specific recipe, a silicone madeleine pan can be used, as it will be easier to unmold the glazed madeleines from a silicone pan than from a metal one.

HONEY MADELEINES

Madeleines are often lightly sweetened with honey, but for this recipe, honey is used both for sweetness and taste. The fun part is that you can play around with different types of honey—such as clover, acacia or mānuka—to create distinctive flavors.

MAKES 12 MADELEINES

50 g unsalted butter, plus soft butter for pan

20 ml whole milk

60 g honey

1 large egg, at room temperature

15 g superfine or granulated sugar

15 ml fresh lemon juice

½ tsp lemon zest

75 g all-purpose flour

1 tsp baking powder

Pinch of fine table salt

1. In a small, microwave-safe bowl, melt the butter in a microwave. Alternatively, melt it in a small saucepan over low heat. Set aside to cool. In a heatproof bowl set atop a saucepan of boiling water (do not let the water touch the bowl), or in a microwave-safe bowl, combine the milk and honey and heat/microwave for a few seconds to melt the honey. Set aside. In a large bowl, whisk together the egg and sugar for 3 to 4 minutes; the mixture should have almost doubled in volume, and look paler and thicker. Mix in the honey mixture, lemon juice and zest. Add the flour, baking powder and salt, and mix until smooth. Lastly, add the cooled melted butter and whisk until you get a smooth, thick batter. Cover the bowl with plastic wrap touching the surface of the batter and refrigerate for at least 3 hours, preferably overnight.

2. Generously butter a metal madeleine pan with soft butter. Transfer the batter to a piping bag and cut the tip to create a small opening. Pipe the batter into the prepared pan, filling each mold no more than halfway. Alternatively, simply scoop small dollops of batter in the prepared pan. It is better to bake a second batch separately rather than to overfill the pan.

3. Place the filled madeleine pan in the fridge and preheat your oven to 390°F (200°C). Bake for 3 minutes, lower the temperature to 350°F (180°C) and bake for an additional 4 to 6 minutes. The edges should be lightly golden and the center should have risen into a tall bump. Let cool completely in the pan on a wire rack before removing from the pan.

PRO TIP: Use a honey that has a naturally strong and rich flavor for the best madeleine taste. Darker-colored honey—such as Mānuka or Buckwheat Honey—tend to have a stronger flavor than lighter ones like Clover or Acacia.

PRALINÉ-FILLED MADELEINES

In this recipe, sweet nutty pâte de praliné flavors the madeleine batter and is also piped into the baked cakes to reveal an oozing center when you bite into it. The same technique can be used with a variety of fillings, such as jams or compotes!

MAKES 12 MADELEINES

....

1.   In a small, microwave-safe bowl, melt the butter in a micro-wave. Alternatively, melt it in a small saucepan over low heat. Set aside to cool. In a large bowl, combine the egg and sugar and whisk together for 3 to 4 minutes; the mixture should have almost doubled in volume, and look paler and thicker. Mix in the milk and 50 g of the pâte de praliné, then the flour, almond meal, baking powder and salt. Add the melted butter and mix until smooth, then cover with plastic wrap touching the surface of the batter and refrigerate for at least 3 hours, preferably overnight.

2.   Generously butter a metal madeleine pan with soft butter. Transfer the batter to a piping bag and cut the tip to create a small opening. Pipe the batter into the prepared pan, filling each mold no more than halfway. Alternatively, simply scoop small dollops of batter into the prepared pan. It is better to bake a second batch separately rather than to overfill the pan.

3.   Place the filled madeleine pan in the fridge and preheat your oven to 390°F (200°C). Bake for 3 minutes, lower the temperature to 350°F (180°C) and bake for an additional 5 minutes. The edges should be lightly golden and the center should have risen into a tall bump. Let cool completely on a wire rack before removing from the pan.

4.   Place the remaining 75 g of pâte de praliné in a piping bag and cut the tip to create a very small opening. With a knife, poke a small hole on top of each madeleine. Place the piping bag through the opening and pipe in the pâte de praliné until it starts to come out.

50 g unsalted butter, plus soft butter for pan

1 large egg, at room temperature

30 g light brown sugar

40 ml whole milk

125 g Pâte de Praliné (page 20), divided

60 g all-purpose flour

15 g almond meal

1 tsp baking powder

Pinch of fine table salt

BASIC ALMOND FINANCIERS

A financier (originally called *visitandine*) is a small tea cake made with almond meal and egg whites. They mainly rely on the almond and *beurre-noisette* (brown butter) for flavor. They are traditionally baked in a shallow rectangular pan that makes the cake look like a bar of gold, which could explain the origin of their name. They can be enjoyed plain in their most basic form or flavored with fruits, coffee, chocolate, different nuts and more!

MAKES 12 FINANCIERS

Melted butter or neutral oil, for pan

110 g unsalted butter

25 g all-purpose flour

100 g almond meal

75 g powdered sugar

Pinch of fine table salt

4 large egg whites (about 120 g)

50 g flaked almonds (optional)

1. Preheat your oven to 325°F (160°C). Butter or oil a financier pan. If you don't have a financier pan, use an eight-well mini loaf pan or a 12-well muffin pan.

2. Prepare the brown butter: In a small saucepan, heat the butter over medium-low heat. Cook for about 5 minutes, or until the melted butter has turned golden and releases a nutty aroma. Remove from the heat as soon as small brown specks appear at the bottom of the saucepan, to prevent burning it, and set aside to cool.

3. Into a large bowl, sift together the all-purpose flour, almond meal, powdered sugar and salt. Set aside.

4. In a small bowl, lightly whisk the egg whites for about 1 minute, or until small bubbles appear. Then, add the egg whites to the flour mixture and whisk until smooth. Mix in the cooled brown butter.

5. Scoop the batter into the prepared financier pan and top with the flaked almonds (if using). Bake for 12 to 14 minutes, or until the edges are lightly golden. Remove from the oven and place the pan on a wire rack to cool for 15 minutes before removing the cakes from the pan. Use a small, blunt knife to lift the cakes out of the pan, if needed. Allow to cool completely before serving.

PRO TIP: Keep the egg yolks for another recipe, such as my Coconut Crèmes Brûlées (page 133).

STRAWBERRY FINANCIERS

Nothing comes close to the scent of oven-roasted strawberries . . . and this is exactly what you get with these strawberry financiers! This recipe shows you how easy it is to flavor a basic financier cake with the fruit of your choice by simply adding it on top of the batter before you bake it.

MAKES 12 FINANCIERS

Melted butter or neutral oil, for pan

110 g unsalted butter

150 g fresh strawberries

40 g all-purpose flour

100 g almond meal

75 g powdered sugar

Pinch of fine table salt

4 large egg whites (about 120 g)

1. Preheat your oven to 325°F (160°C). Butter or oil a financier pan. If you don't have a financier pan, use an eight-well mini loaf pan or a 12-well standard muffin pan.

2. Prepare the brown butter: In a small saucepan, heat the butter over medium-low heat. Cook for about 5 minutes, or until the butter turns golden, releases a nutty aroma and small brown specks appear at the bottom of the saucepan. Remove from the heat and set aside to cool.

3. Wash, hull and slice the strawberries into very small cubes, each about ¼ inch (8 mm). Set aside. Into a large bowl, sift together the all-purpose flour, almond meal, powdered sugar and salt. Set aside.

4. In a small bowl, lightly whisk the egg whites for about 1 minute, or until small bubbles appear. Then, add the egg whites to the flour mixture and whisk until smooth. Mix in the cooled brown butter.

5. Scoop the batter into the prepared financier pan, then generously top each cake with the cubed strawberries, leaving the edges bare. Bake for 12 to 14 minutes, or until the edges are lightly golden. Remove from the oven and place the pan on a wire rack to cool completely before removing the cakes from the pan. Use a small, blunt knife to lift the cakes out of the pan, if needed.

LEMON POPPY SEED FINANCIERS

Financiers are naturally soft and moist cakes, so loading them with poppy seeds is a great way to add some extra crunch. Lemon and poppy seeds is a classic flavor combination that works so well with the nutty taste of almonds. For even stronger lemon flavor, you can brush the top of the cakes with a lemon syrup when they are still slightly warm.

MAKES 12 FINANCIERS

....

1. Preheat your oven to 325°F (160°C). Butter or oil a financier pan. If you don't have a financier pan, use an eight-well mini loaf pan or a 12-well standard muffin pan.

2. Prepare the brown butter: In a small saucepan, heat the butter over medium-low heat. Cook for about 5 minutes, or until the butter turns golden, releases a nutty aroma and small brown specks appear at the bottom of the saucepan. Remove from the heat and set aside to cool.

3. Into a large bowl, sift together all-purpose flour, almond meal, powdered sugar and salt. Mix in the poppy seeds and set aside.

4. In a small bowl, lightly whisk the egg whites for about 1 minute, or until small bubbles appear. Then, add the egg whites to the flour mixture along with the lemon zest and juice. Whisk until smooth, then mix in the cooled brown butter.

5. Scoop the batter into the prepared financier pan. Bake for 12 to 14 minutes, or until the edges are lightly golden. Remove from the oven and place the pan on a wire rack to cool for 15 minutes before removing the cakes from the pan. Use a small, blunt knife to lift the cakes out of the pan if needed. Let cool completely before serving.

Melted butter or neutral oil, for pan

110 g unsalted butter

40 g all-purpose flour

100 g almond meal

75 g powdered sugar

Pinch of fine table salt

12 g poppy seeds

4 large egg whites (about 120 g)

6 g lemon zest (from about 2 lemons)

30 ml fresh lemon juice

ORANGE HAZELNUT FINANCIERS

Although financiers are traditionally made with almonds, replacing them with hazelnuts is a delicious way to give the classic a twist. The deep, earthy flavor of hazelnuts is brightened by a delicate touch of fresh orange here. No need to make brown butter; the hazelnuts add all the nuttiness you need!

MAKES 12 FINANCIERS

Melted butter or neutral oil, for pan

85 g unsalted butter

30 g all-purpose flour

100 g hazelnut meal

75 g powdered sugar

Pinch of fine table salt

4 large egg whites (about 120 g)

6 g orange zest (from about 2 large oranges)

30 ml fresh orange juice

2 orange slices, to garnish

1. Preheat your oven to 325°F (160°C). Butter or oil a financier pan. If you don't have a financier pan, use an eight-well mini loaf pan or a 12-well standard muffin pan. In a small, microwave-safe bowl, melt the butter in a microwave. Alternatively, melt it in a small saucepan over low heat. Set aside to cool.

2. Into a large bowl, sift together all-purpose flour, hazelnut meal, powdered sugar and salt. Set aside.

3. In a small bowl, lightly whisk the egg whites for 1 minute, or until small bubbles appear. Then, add the egg whites, orange zest and orange juice to the flour mixture and mix until combined. Whisk in the cooled melted butter until you get a smooth batter.

4. Scoop the batter into the prepared financier pan. Cut each orange slice into six equal segments and place one on top of each financier.

5. Bake for 12 to 14 minutes, or until the edges of the financiers are very lightly golden. Remove from the oven and place the pan on a wire rack to cool for 15 minutes before removing the cakes from the pan. Use a small, blunt knife to lift the cakes out of the pan, if needed. Let cool completely before serving.

TIGRÉS FINANCIERS

The word *tigré* ("striped like a tiger") simply describes the pattern created by adding finely chopped chocolate to a basic financier. Tigrés are baked in a mini savarin or kugelhopf pan (I use a mini Bundt pan here). The hollow center is then filled with a chocolate ganache.

MAKES 12 FINANCIERS

1. Preheat your oven to 325°F (160°C). Generously brush the inside of a 12-well mini Bundt pan, savarin pan or fluted tube pan with oil or melted butter.

2. Prepare the brown butter: In a small saucepan, heat the butter over medium-low heat. Cook for about 5 minutes, or until the butter has turned golden, releases a nutty aroma and small brown specks appear at the bottom of the saucepan. Remove from the heat and set aside to cool.

3. Into a large bowl, sift together the all-purpose flour, almond meal, powdered sugar and salt. In a small bowl, lightly whisk the egg whites for about 1 minute, or until small bubbles appear. Then, add the egg whites to the flour mixture and whisk until combined. Mix in the cooled brown butter to get a smooth batter, then fold in the chocolate.

4. Pour the batter into the prepared pan and bake for 12 to 14 minutes, or until the top is lightly golden. Remove from the oven, place the pan on a wire rack to cool for 15 minutes, then flip the plan to release the financiers. Let cool completely.

5. Prepare the ganache filling: In a heatproof bowl set atop a saucepan of boiling water (do not let the water touch the bowl), heat the chocolate for 30 seconds to 1 minute, or until the bottom of the chocolate has started to melt slightly. Remove from the heat. Meanwhile, in a separate small saucepan over low heat, heat the cream. When it starts to simmer, pour it over the chocolate. Leave for 2 minutes, then gently stir with a spatula until it comes together into a smooth, shiny ganache. Pour inside the cavity of each financier and let set for 1 to 2 hours.

FINANCIERS

Neutral oil or melted butter, for pan

150 g unsalted butter

30 g all-purpose flour

125 g almond meal

100 g powdered sugar

Pinch of fine table salt

5 large egg whites (about 150 g)

40 g dark baking chocolate, chopped very finely

CHOCOLATE GANACHE FILLING

65 g dark baking chocolate, chopped finely

65 ml heavy cream

PRO TIP: Make sure that the brown butter is completely cool before mixing it into the batter. If it is still warm, it will make the chocolate chunks melt.

INDIVIDUAL DESSERTS

No proper French meal is finished without dessert. Although many French people will opt for cheese, I've always been on "team sweet."

A lot of the desserts you will find in this chapter are custard-based: Custards are amazingly versatile. They can be used as sauces or fillings when just cooked on the stove, such as a Crème Pâtissière (page 16), or be baked in the oven to create velvety, creamy desserts, such as Coconut Crèmes Brûlées (page 133), Coffee Crèmes Caramel (page 146) or Petits Pots de Crème (pages 134 and 137). These last desserts use a *crème anglaise* base, which is a specific type of custard that does not contain cornstarch or flour and is much runnier than a crème pâtissière.

Other desserts in this chapter are what I would call *desserts d'enfance*, or "childhood desserts." They are easy, comforting, nostalgic desserts, such as Mini Cherry Clafoutis (page 129) or Mousse au Chocolat Cups (page 138). The ones you can eat over and over again and never get tired of!

French desserts can also be as simple as poached fruits—although those always come with a twist. Poached pears are topped with a decadent dark chocolate sauce to make Poires Belle-Hélène (page 142), or cooked in fragrant rosé wine to make Rosé Poached Peaches (page 141). This simple cooking technique allows for seasonal fruits to really shine without requiring any baking.

Whichever way you decide to end your meal, make it memorable!

MINI CHERRY CLAFOUTIS

For me, nothing says "lazy Sunday afternoon" like a clafoutis. This type of baked custard topped with fresh cherries is incredibly simple to make. Milk, butter, eggs, sugar and flour are mixed together, poured over cherries in a large baking sheet (or small ramekins for this individual version) and baked until deliciously fluffy and soft. Traditionally, a clafoutis is made with unpitted cherries.

MAKES 6 CLAFOUTIS

1. Preheat your oven to 325°F (160°C). Place six 3½-inch (9-cm) square or 4-inch (10-cm) round ramekins on a baking sheet.

2. In a large bowl, whisk together the eggs, sugar and vanilla until just combined, then mix in the oil. Whisk in the flour and salt until smooth. Pour in the milk and whisk until completely incorporated and lump-free. Pour the mixture into the prepared ramekins and top each with five or six pitted cherries.

3. Bake for 25 minutes, or until very lightly golden. Remove from the oven and allow to cool for 15 minutes and dust with powdered sugar (if using) before serving.

2 large eggs

50 g superfine or granulated sugar

1 tsp vanilla extract

15 ml canola or other neutral oil

50 g all-purpose flour, sifted

Pinch of fine table salt

250 ml whole milk

300 g pitted cherries (or 400 g unpitted for the traditional recipe)

Powdered sugar, for serving (optional)

PRO TIP: Clafoutis can be made in advance and kept in the fridge for a day. Slightly reheat in the oven or microwave before serving.

MINI PEAR FLAUGNARDES

Flaugnarde is the name given to a clafoutis when made with a different fruit than cherries. You can swap in apples, plums or strawberries, for example, but pears are the fruit my mother would use the most often, so this dessert is deliciously nostalgic to me. A touch of lemon zest is added to the batter to bring out the soft flavors of the pear.

MAKES 6 FLAUGNARDES

1 large pear

2 large eggs, at room temperature

50 g superfine or granulated sugar

15 ml canola or other neutral oil

1 tsp lemon zest

50 g all-purpose flour, sifted

Pinch of fine table salt

250 ml whole milk

1. Preheat your oven to 325°F (160°C). Have ready six 3-inch (7.5-cm)-wide ramekins. Peel the pear, remove the core and slice the fruit into ½-inch (1.2-cm) cubes. Divide the cubes equally among the bottoms of the ramekins and set aside.

2. In a large bowl, whisk together the eggs and sugar until just combined, then mix in the oil and lemon zest. Add the flour and salt, and whisk until no lumps remain. Add the milk and whisk until smooth. Evenly pour the mixture over the pear cubes to fill the ramekins almost all the way to the top.

3. Bake for 20 to 25 minutes, or until the top starts to get very lightly golden. Remove from the oven and allow to cool for 15 minutes before serving. If making in advance, reheat until lukewarm before serving.

PRO TIP: Although this recipe does not contain any rising agent, the flaugnardes puff in the oven. Make sure not to overfill the ramekins, or else the batter may overflow.

COCONUT CRÈMES BRÛLÉES

A fun and delicious twist on a classic crème brûlée, this recipe is sweetened with coconut sugar and uses coconut cream instead of traditional heavy cream. Although crèmes brûlées are often baked in a bain-marie, baking them at a low temperature for a longer time instead gives them the silkiest, softest custardy texture without the fuss. It is a great dessert for a fancy dinner party: super easy to prepare and guaranteed to impress your guests!

MAKES 6 CRÈMES BRÛLÉES

1. Prepare the coconut custard: Preheat your oven to 100°C (215°F).

2. In a small saucepan, combine the coconut cream and vanilla paste and heat over low heat. In the meantime, in a small heat-proof bowl, whisk together the egg yolks and coconut sugar until just combined. Once the cream starts to simmer, slowly pour it over the egg yolk mixture while continuously mixing.

3. Pour the custard into six 5-inch (12.5-cm)-diameter round baking dishes. Tap each dish against a hard surface to pop any air bubbles. Bake for 40 to 45 minutes; the middle of each crème brûlée should still be very slightly wobbly.

4. Remove from the oven, place on a wire rack and let cool at room temperature for 1 hour, then chill in the fridge for at least 2 hours, or until ready to serve.

5. Prepare the caramelized shell: Sprinkle ½ teaspoon of sugar over each crème brûlée. Gently shake and tilt the dishes to evenly distribute the sugar in an even layer. With a kitchen torch, caramelize the sugar until it starts to bubble and turns to an amber color. Try not to apply the flame directly onto the sugar, or it might burn. Alternatively, place under the hot oven broiler for about a minute, or until the sugar starts to caramelize. Make sure to keep an eye on the dessert, as it could burn quickly depending on the temperature of your broiler.

6. Place in the freezer for 15 minutes to allow for the shell to harden and for the custard to set again. Serve immediately.

COCONUT CUSTARD

360 ml canned coconut cream

1 tsp vanilla paste

4 large egg yolks, at room temperature

45 g coconut sugar

CARAMELIZED SHELL

15 g superfine or granulated sugar

> **PRO TIP:** If you don't have these specific baking dishes, you can use regular 3-inch (7.5-cm) ramekins and bake the crèmes brûlées for 55 to 60 minutes.

LEMON PETITS POTS DE CRÈME

Petits pots de crème are a popular dessert in France. Although you can find them in the supermarket, these baked custards are surprisingly easy to make at home. They are baked in a bain-marie at low temperature to create a super soft, creamy (and irresistible) texture. They are flavored simply with lemon for a super fresh dessert.

MAKES 6 POTS

240 ml heavy cream

120 ml fresh lemon juice

2 tsp lemon zest (from about 2 large lemons)

4 large eggs, at room temperature

120 g superfine or granulated sugar

1. Preheat your oven to 285°F (140°C). Prepare six 3-inch (7.5-cm)-wide ramekins and a deep baking dish or roasting pan.

2. In a small saucepan, combine the cream and lemon juice. Stir and bring to a simmer over low heat. In the meantime, in a large bowl, combine the lemon zest, eggs and sugar. Whisk until just mixed; you don't want to create any bubbles. When the cream mixture is warm, slowly pour it over the egg mixture while stirring. Continue to stir until fully combined and smooth. Use a slotted spoon to remove any foam or bubbles that might have formed on top.

3. Evenly pour the mixture into the ramekins and tap each ramekin against a hard surface to pop any leftover air bubbles. Place the ramekins inside the prepared baking dish or roasting pan and fill it with warm (but not boiling) water going about halfway up outside of the ramekins (this is called making a bain-marie), then place carefully in the oven.

4. Bake for 25 to 30 minutes; the edges should have set but the center should still be very slightly jiggly. Remove carefully from the oven (the water will be very hot) and leave inside the bain-marie for 10 minutes. Remove the ramekins carefully from the baking dish and leave at room temperature for another 15 minutes, then chill in the fridge for at least 1 hour, or until completely cool.

PRO TIP: The pots de crème will continue to set as they cool. Make sure to stop baking before they're completely set, or they will get a slightly rubbery consistency.

SALTED CARAMEL PETITS POTS DE CRÈME

This recipe is a fun cross between a petit pot de crème and a crème caramel. You get the deliciously soft and creamy texture of a petit pot de crème with the same deep flavors of salted caramel compared to the milder-tasting crème caramel.

MAKES 6 POT

1. Prepare the caramel: In a small saucepan, combine the sugar and water. Place over medium-low heat and allow to cook for 8 to 10 minutes without touching the sugar. The sugar should have completely melted and turned a light amber color. Meanwhile, in a separate small saucepan, heat half of the cream over low heat until warm. When the sugar reaches the desired color, remove from the heat and carefully pour in the warm cream while stirring. The caramel will bubble and rise quickly. Continue to stir until you get a smooth liquid consistency. Mix in the remaining (cold) cream and flaky sea salt. Set aside to cool for 10 to 15 minutes.

2. Preheat your oven to 285°F (140°C). Prepare six 3-inch (7.5-cm)-wide ramekins and a deep baking dish or roasting pan.

3. Make the custard: In a large heatproof bowl, lightly whisk the eggs and sugar until just combined. Mix in the cooled caramel sauce to get a glossy, thick batter.

4. Evenly pour the custard into the ramekins and gently tap each ramekin on a hard surface to pop any air bubbles. Place the ramekins in the large baking dish and pour in some warm water about halfway up around the ramekins. Bake for 25 to 30 minutes; the center should still be slightly jiggly.

5. Carefully remove from the oven (the water will be very hot) and remove the ramekins from the bain-marie. Let cool at room temperature for 30 minutes, then chill in the fridge for at least 1 hour, or until completely cool and set. They can also be enjoyed slightly warm for a creamier, less set consistency.

CARAMEL

150 g superfine or granulated sugar

30 ml water

360 ml heavy cream, divided in two

½ tsp flaky sea salt

CUSTARD

4 large eggs, at room temperature

50 g superfine or granulated sugar

MOUSSE AU CHOCOLAT CUPS

It doesn't get more classic or more comforting than chocolate mousse. The darker the chocolate, the better—which is why I recommend using a 70% cacao chocolate. This recipe follows a traditional method using raw eggs. But do not worry—fresh pasteurized eggs are completely fine to be eaten raw!

MAKES 6 CHOCOLATE CUPS

1. In a heatproof bowl set atop a saucepan of boiling water (do not let the water touch the bowl), or in a microwave-safe bowl microwaving in 30-second increments, melt the chocolate. Remove from the heat and stir in the lukewarm cream until smooth. Mix in small cubes of butter, a little at a time, until fully melted. The chocolate shouldn't feel hot to the touch anymore.

2. Add the egg yolks to the bowl of melted chocolate and whisk until combined, then set aside. In a large bowl, using an electric hand mixer, or in the bowl of a stand mixer fitted with the whisk attachment, combine the egg whites and salt. Whip the egg whites on medium speed until you get soft peaks (the egg whites should have thickened, doubled in size and turned white). Start adding the sugar, a little at a time, while continuously whisking. Once all the sugar has been added, increase the speed to high and keep whisking until you get stiff peaks. The egg whites should be very thick, stiff and slightly glossy.

3. Add a little of the whisked egg whites to the melted chocolate mixture and whisk well to loosen the chocolate. Switch to a spatula and very gently fold in the rest of the egg whites in four or five batches, until fully incorporated. Be careful not to overmix, or you risk deflating the egg whites.

4. Pour the chocolate mousse into six serving cups and chill in the fridge for at least 2 hours. Top with dark chocolate shavings before serving.

150 g dark baking chocolate, 70% cacao, chopped finely

45 ml heavy cream, lukewarm

45 g unsalted butter, cut into small cubes

5 large pasteurized eggs, separated

¼ tsp fine table salt

50 g superfine or granulated sugar

30 g dark chocolate shavings

PRO TIP: Ingredient temperatures are very important in creating the right mousse texture. If the chocolate is too hot when you add the egg yolks, it will cook them and make it curdle. If the egg yolks are too cold, it will make the chocolate seize.

ROSÉ POACHED PEACHES

Poaching is an easy cooking method that involves cooking an ingredient (a fruit, here) in a liquid at a relatively low temperature. Red wine is often used to poach fruits in winter, but this summery version is made with peaches and fresh rosé wine. The leftover poaching liquid is reduced into a decadent, thick syrup to serve over the fruits because we never waste anything!

6 fresh peaches, ripe but slightly firm

1 orange

500 ml rosé wine

100 g superfine or granulated sugar

MAKES 6 POACHED PEACHES

1. Wash the peaches, slice them in half and remove their stones. Set aside.

2. Using a peeler, cut off the skin of the orange, trying to omit all the pith. Juice the orange; you should have 80 ml of juice. Place the peels in a medium-sized saucepan along with the juice of the orange, rosé wine and sugar. Gently stir to mix, then place over medium heat.

3. Once the liquid starts to boil, lower the heat to medium-low and add the halved peaches. Let simmer for 20 to 25 minutes, or until the fruit is very soft. Occasionally turn the peaches around so that both sides are cooked evenly.

4. Remove the poached peaches from the saucepan and place two halves on each serving plate or bowl.

5. Make the syrup: Increase the heat under the remaining liquid and orange peels in the saucepan to medium and let simmer for 15 to 20 minutes, or until most of the syrup has reduced and is very slightly thick and sticky. Pour the syrup and now candied orange peels over the poached peaches and serve warm.

PRO TIP #1: The exact poaching time varies based on how firm or ripe the peaches are. Cook for a shorter or longer time, if needed; the fruits should be soft but still hold their shape.

PRO TIP #2: Depending on the size of your saucepan and of your peaches, you might need to add a little bit more rosé to make sure the peaches are fully submerged in the poaching liquid.

POIRES BELLE-HÉLÈNE

This is another "grand classic" of French pastry created by legendary chef Auguste Escoffier, named in honor of the Offenbach operetta *La Belle Hélène*. Pears are poached in a syrup—here, lightly flavored with lemon and vanilla—and then topped with a warm chocolate sauce and toasted almonds. And if you feel particularly decadent, you can even serve it with a scoop of vanilla ice cream!

MAKES 6 PEARS

1. Make the poached pears: Peel the pears (keeping the stem on) and set aside. In a very large saucepan, combine the water, lemon juice, sugar and vanilla paste. Bring to a simmer over medium-low heat, then add the pears. If needed, add a little bit more water to fully submerge the pears in liquid. Cook covered with the lid on for 15 minutes, then without the lid for another 10 to 15 minutes, or until the pears are slightly soft. Transfer the pears onto a wire rack lined with paper towels and let cool for 10 to 15 minutes. You can slice off the bottom of the pears to allow them to stand easily.

2. Spread the flaked almonds on a baking sheet lined with parchment paper or a silicone mat. Bake for about 5 minutes at 350°F (180°C), or until the almonds start to turn golden. Set aside.

3. In a heatproof bowl set atop a saucepan of boiling water (do not let the water touch the bowl), or in a microwave-safe bowl, microwaving for 30 seconds to 1 minute, heat the chocolate until the bottom starts to turn soft. In a separate small saucepan, heat the milk over low heat until it simmers, then pour over the chocolate. Gently stir until the chocolate is completely melted and you get a smooth sauce.

4. To serve, place each poached pear on a serving plate. Pour the warm chocolate sauce over each pear and top with the roasted flaked almonds. Serve immediately.

POACHED PEARS

6 Bosc or Anjou pears

1.5 L water

30 ml fresh lemon juice

100 g superfine or granulated sugar

1 tsp vanilla paste

FOR ASSEMBLY

25 g flaked almonds

120 g dark baking chocolate, chopped finely

80 ml whole milk

PRO TIP: Once the poached pears have cooled slightly, you can flip them over and carve out the inside to remove the core.

COULANTS AU CHOCOLAT

If there is one dessert you are sure to find on every French restaurant menu, it's a coulant au chocolat (sometimes called *mi-cuit, moelleux* or *fondant au chocolat*). The center of the warm chocolate cake oozes with melting, slightly underbaked chocolate batter in a dramatic and oh-so-decadent fashion. It is an impressive dessert to serve at a dinner party—and no one will guess how easy it is to prepare!

MAKES 6 COULANTS

Soft butter, for pan

150 g dark baking chocolate, chopped finely

100 g unsalted butter

4 large eggs, at room temperature

50 g superfine or granulated sugar

40 g all-purpose flour, sifted

Pinch of fine table salt

1. Preheat your oven to 350°F (180°C). Generously butter six 3-inch (7.5-cm)-wide ramekins with soft butter.

2. In a heatproof bowl set atop a saucepan of boiling water (do not let the water touch the bowl), or in a microwave-safe bowl microwaving in 30-second increments, melt the chocolate and butter until completely smooth. Set aside to cool.

3. In a separate bowl, whisk together the eggs and sugar until just combined. Mix in the melted chocolate mixture, then the flour and salt. Evenly pour the batter into the prepared ramekins.

4. Bake for 8 to 10 minutes. The center of the cakes should still be quite soft and slightly jiggly. Place the ramekins on a wire rack to cool for 5 minutes. Cover each ramekin with a small serving plate and carefully flip upside down to release the cakes onto the plates. If the cakes don't come out, run a knife around the edges. Serve immediately.

PRO TIP: The batter can be made in advance, poured into the ramekins and kept in the fridge for up to 2 hours. Allow them to come back to room temperature for 30 minutes before baking them.

COFFEE CRÈMES CARAMEL

A crème caramel, sometimes called *crème renversée au caramel* (upside-down caramel cream), is a custard-based dessert baked on top of a layer of caramel. Once chilled, the dessert is flipped upside down to reveal a liquid layer of caramel that drips over the super soft baked custard. This dessert is similar to a flan.

MAKES 6 CRÈMES CARAMEL

1. Preheat your oven to 285°F (140°C). Prepare six 3-inch (7.5-cm)-wide ramekins and a deep baking dish or roasting pan.

2. Prepare the caramel: In a small saucepan, combine the sugar and water. Without mixing or touching the sugar, heat over medium heat and leave for 8 to 10 minutes, or until the sugar has completely melted and turned a light amber color. Directly pour the warm caramel evenly inside the ramekins and set aside to harden. If the caramel sets before you finish pouring it into the ramekins, place it back on the stove for a few seconds to melt it again.

3. Make the custard: In a small saucepan, combine the milk and instant coffee. Whisk to mix, then place over low heat. Meanwhile, in a heatproof bowl, whisk together the sugar and eggs until just combined. When the milk starts to simmer, slowly pour the milk mixture over the egg mixture while continuously mixing until smooth. Pour the mixture through a fine-mesh sieve into a large heatproof pitcher or liquid measuring cup with a lip, to remove any bubbles or bits of unmixed eggs.

(CONTINUED)

CARAMEL
80 g superfine or granulated sugar

15 ml water

COFFEE CUSTARD
500 ml whole milk

9 g instant coffee granules

60 g superfine or granulated sugar

3 large eggs, at room temperature

COFFEE CRÈMES CARAMEL (CONTINUED)

4. Pour the custard evenly over the hardened caramel in the ramekins. Gently tap each ramekin on a hard surface to pop any leftover air bubbles, then place inside the large baking dish. Pour warm (but not boiling) water inside the baking dish, filling it about halfway up around the ramekins. Place carefully in the oven.

5. Bake for 30 to 35 minutes. The custard should be still slightly jiggly in its center and the tip of a knife should come out clean. Remove carefully from the oven (the water will be hot) and carefully remove the ramekins from the water bath, using oven mitts. Let cool at room temperature for 30 minutes, then chill in the fridge for 1 hour, or until completely cool. Run a small, sharp knife around the edges of the ramekins, place an upside-down plate on top of a ramekin and flip it over to release the crème caramel.

PRO TIP: If the crème caramel won't release from the ramekin, it is usually a sign that the caramel layer at the bottom has hardened too much. To release the custard, dip the bottom of each ramekin in a bowl of warm water for a couple of minutes to soften the caramel before flipping it over a plate.

ACKNOWLEDGMENTS

This book would have not been possible without the unlimited support from my husband, Ariel. Thank you for tasting all of these recipes *multiple times*—even when you were begging me to stop feeding you sweets—and providing essential feedback.

I would also like to thank all my family—in both Australia and Europe—for your never-ending encouragement and excitement around the book—and the well-needed help with my son, Noah. Constantly feeding you is the best way I know to show you my love!

A particular thank-you goes to my mum, who proofread my original manuscript even though she is not fully fluent in English.

To all of my friends who are my biggest cheerleaders, thank you for believing in me!

To our favorite neighbors who happily ate kilos and kilos of cakes over the last few months—thank you for your positivity and love.

Lastly, I would like to thank Page Street Publishing—and my editor, Madeline, in particular—for giving me the opportunity to create this book and supporting it along the way. It will forever be one of my proudest achievements!

ABOUT THE AUTHOR

Sylvie grew up in Belgium with her French mum, Belgian father and brother, Jeremie. After getting a master's degree in architecture, she moved to Melbourne, Australia, in 2014. In 2018, she decided to quit her job as an architect and start her blog A Baking Journey. The blog focuses on well-detailed and easy-to-follow recipes with a French touch. Sylvie is passionate about teaching pastry to home bakers of any skill level and always encourages her students to try more challenging recipes while having fun in the kitchen. In 2019, she achieved one of her life dreams of attending pastry school in Paris at École Ducasse.

Sylvie lives in Melbourne with her husband, Ariel; her son, Noah; and their dog, Luna.

INDEX